MW00719117

Little Women Hospitality Program

by

Anne Milligan Callaghan

Teacher's Manual

**Cover illustrations by
Patrick J. Callaghan and Julia Fahy**

Other books programs available through Ecce Homo Press:

Little Flowers Girls' Club Program

Blue Knights Boys' Club Program

The Glory of America Series

www.eccehomopress.com

Any omission of credits is unintentional. The publisher requests documentation for future printings.

ISBN: 978-0-9797609-1-4
ISBN 10:0-9797609-1-7
Copyright 2008 Ecce Homo Press
All rights reserved

No portion of this manual may be reproduced without expressed written consent of publisher

Dedicated to my generous and loving family who supported, encouraged and helped me through all the parts of this program: For my husband, Jerry, and my children Nicholas, Patrick, Catherine, Sean, Ben and Marty. Thank you.

Introduction

The Little Women Hospitality Program is a unique Catholic girls program that teaches girls how to become young ladies. It will equip young girls with a love for the virtue of hospitality, an understanding of what it means to serve others, and a practical way, through everyday skills, to accomplish this.

Hospitality is a virtue that teaches us how to treat and love others. It helps us to be compassionate, generous, kind and considerate as we serve them. Therefore, this program follows the same model we have in our own lives, the model which brings richness and a sense of purpose to all that we do. Our Lord said, "Upon this rock I build my Church." He taught us that we must have a strong foundation for anything we do or it will get washed away with the sand. The basis of our lives is the same foundation He gave to us over 2000 years ago: His Church and the gift of Faith. This should permeate everything we do. It does not mean that we should be on a soap box preaching the gospel to everyone we see. It means that we should give our best in all that we do each day, because we are striving for perfection and the Kingdom of Heaven. We must enjoy others and see Christ in those we meet.

Often in this busy world, Faith becomes just another compartment in our life, something we practice on Sunday, when it should be the foundation upon which everything else stands. When we work, we should offer it as a prayer that all that we do is good and honest. When we do our school work, we should do our best, and if there are difficulties, ask for help. It does not mean we will get everything perfect, just that we must give our all. When we are with our children, we should be patient and kind. When we vacation, we should pick a trip that will be refreshing and fun, but be careful not to pick a place that may offend Our Lord. This is what it means to let our Faith bring formation to our lives. Our Faith should not only be reflected in our daily lives, but also give strength to it.

This program helps our girls to see this gentle way of living, through learning the values and skills of hospitality. It shows them that to do a job well is only half a job. It must be done joyfully with a love for those it is meant to serve. Someone can clean a room because they were asked to, and do it perfectly, but if he/she was mad the entire time, the task has very little spiritual reward. A girl may help watch her siblings for her mom, but complain while doing it. The spiritual foundation is the basis for our lives. This is clearly shared with the girls as they become proficient in everyday skills. Going through the motions of life without Faith will not build a strong house. We want our girls to grow into true little women. Hopefully, this program will help the girls and all of us, to strengthen our foundations as we strive for Heaven.

This program is filled with wonderful stories, inspiring heroes, saints, Biblical figures, and practical skills that will enrich our lives and make each day easier. As a girl, I remember learning to square a corner on a bed and other skills as I joined a group of girls for an afternoon of fun and friendship. I loved these meetings and wanted our girls to enjoy this same sort of gathering.

Bringing this virtue to my adult life, my family has entertained others on several occasions including a yearly historical party in honor of St. Nicholas. A dear friend of ours, a guest at these parties, has returned the gesture on several occasions inviting us into her home for an evening of fine china, well-prepared food, good conversation and lovely surroundings. Once I commented to her how well she practiced the virtue of hospitality. She only responded, "Hospitality is a virtue? I didn't know that." What a wonderful new door had been opened to her. She had never been told that the things we do to serve others, whether entertaining in our home, keeping a house for our family, practicing any of the corporal works of mercy or just being a true friend, are all parts of a more spiritual calling.

This call is to the virtue of hospitality. Our Lord calls us to serve others and seek out their needs. "Do unto others as you would have them do unto you." (Mt. 7:12) "The least you did to any of my brothers, you did unto me." (Mt. 25:45) I want all our girls to learn this as well. This is what has called me to write this program. The call to hospitality is for each of us, each day, in every circumstance. It is a beautiful way to help fortify our faith as our foundation in all that we do. I hope that our "little women" will get a head start to learn what this means as they enjoy good literature, an inspiring story and a new skill each month while building friendships that will last a lifetime.

Table of Contents

The Nuts and Bolts of the Little Women Hospitality Program

"Offer hospitality to one another...." 1 Peter 4:9

Introduction for Coordinators: The following explains the parts of the manual. This program is set up so all the moms and girls can participate. All girls like to have functions at their home but it can be overwhelming to volunteer to run an entire program. This program is written so everyone can have a turn. The months will rotate houses and hostesses. Since different moms have different strengths, rotating can only add to the lessons. Each month is clearly laid out and defined for the teaching mom so she will feel comfortable knowing exactly what she needs to do, including a time table of how long each section should take. Of course, if one mom wants to teach and host every month, the program will be taught exactly the same way. There are supplies needed each month that can often be found in the context of one's home, so each hostess should have them. There are others that have been specified for the hostess, but as coordinator, you may want to invest in a few group supplies for the year. These would include a set for 12 of paper dishes, dinner, salad and dessert plates, bowls, plastic silverware and cups. These are used in several exercises from table setting and serving to table manners. You may even want to put a disposable camera with the supplies for the hostess to take a picture each month. This will build a nice memory for everyone by the end of the year.

Introduction to Parents: The following program, to teach the virtue and skills of hospitality, is broken into several parts. First, there is a letter that is to be copied and distributed to all parents that explains the heart and soul of the program, as well as the nuts and bolts of it. This letter will help the parents understand what each of their daughters is learning. It also includes a family blessing as a way to root this virtue in the heart of the family itself. The letter will further explain the format and practical level of the program so they can follow along. The table of contents is listed in the student companion book as well for moms to keep track of what the girls are doing each month.

The Teaching Manual: This manual should be kept in a binder with pockets that should also include emails and a phone tree list for your group. These are important for the hostess to contact the members for reminders of material needed and any scheduled field trips. It would be easiest if the coordinator would send out email reminders for the girls each month. It makes everything run smoother if one mom keeps track and overviews the program, although it is designed for moms to share the responsibility of teaching it. There may even be a separate field trip mom who schedules all field trips, and then emails (or calls) everyone with the details.

The TAKE HOME: This is the assignment page in the girls' companion book to the program. It contains a list of ideas and ways to practice the skill of the month. The ideas are fun and provide a way of fostering friendship, culture and family ties. Some activities are corporal works of mercy. These will bring into practice the core meaning of the program: to use our skills to serve others. The TAKE HOME also includes suggestions for field trips that can be coordinated by the hosting mom for the month. They might also be coordinated by a mom who has not signed up to host any particular month. Some of the field trips showcase professionals performing the skills that the girls are learning. Others enable the group to practice the virtue together, as, for instance, in preparing a St. Joseph Table. Lastly, the TAKE HOME includes book recommendations based on the passage of literature read that month, and occasionally, a movie recommendation.

Binders: It would be ideal if the girls kept their books in a 3-ring binder, separated by simple index dividers, into 10 sections, one for each skill. They could include paper protector sheets or photo pages to include recipes, tips, photos, or other things they collect, exchange or discover about hospitality. There are guest pages and other things that the girls make in the program that should be filed in this binder under the listed skill. This will then be a central place for their skills that they can use and keep as they grow. If you provide the binders, as the coordinator, you can copy the cover of their companion book to slide in the front to make it a nice set.

Notes to the Hostess: Each month contains notes to the hostess, giving an overview of the lesson and any special instructions, followed by all the things the hostess will need that month. This program also contains a letter to the hostess to explain how her particular lesson fits into the whole.

Field Trips: Each month has field trips listed that pertain to the skill that month. In the letter to the hostess, it is noted that the teaching mom of the month can plan a field trip for the group. It is also a good option to have a field trip coordinator, a mom who will not be teaching and possibly has more time to put together these types of outings. These outings are important to help the girls foster friendships among themselves. During the lessons, they may not have as much time to get to know each other, but many of the field trips are perfect opportunities for this. They also provide structure for the social gatherings of the girls while they are still getting to know each other. True friendship in today's world is a treasure. Everyone needs to find a "kindred spirit."

The Charms: The charms are earned at the end of each skill and can be given at each meeting, or one or two times a year at an awards ceremony. The charms that go with each skill are: cookie jar: cooking; button: how to clean a room; spoon: setting and clearing a table; circle of friends: table manners and conversation; cabin: preparing a room for a guest; pencil: correspondence; pineapple: bringing hospitality to others; sewing machine: sewing and modesty; tea cup: planning a tea party and book for the book club.

10

Introduction for Parents:

Abraham said, "Let me get you something to eat, so you can be refreshed....." Genesis 18:5

Hospitality is a virtue that has lost its meaning in today's world. It has become a secular term for having a party. Hospitality is not that but a vital means for us as Catholics, especially as women, to serve one another. True hospitality requires generosity. It is the giving of ourselves in ways that few want to give, and requires our love for God to enkindle our love for our neighbor. In living this virtue, we will be living our Lord's call to love our neighbor as our self. "And the King shall answer and say unto them, Verily I say unto you, Inasmuch as ye have done unto one of the least of my brethren, ye have done it unto me." (Matthew 25:40)

Pope John Paul II formed a habit and was an example to us all to reach out to everyone: like or not alike, to make everyone feel welcome and special. He practiced hospitality at its best.

Our Lord calls us to this virtue throughout the Gospels when He gives us His Sermon on the Mount, when he turns water into wine at the wedding at Cana, when he accepts Martha and Mary's hospitality graciously as a good guest. He gives the crowds food for their hearts and souls, but goes further and gives them food for their bodies as well. He visits and comforts the sick, shows compassion for the dying and sorrow for the grieving. These are all ways of extending the virtue of hospitality to others. He provides a resting place for his apostles when they are tired after their journey at sea as He waits for them on shore with a warm fire and fresh fish for their hungry bodies. "...and when they get to land, they saw a charcoal fire there, with fish lying on it, and bread. 'Bring some of the fish that you have just caught,' Jesus said to them.....Jesus said, 'Come and have breakfast.'" (cf: John 21: 10-12) Our Lord does not just call us to hospitality, he shows us how. We can make everyone feel welcome, at home, or in other places, without a lot of complication or expense.

Knowing how to do something is an important part of learning anything. Although the desire to know can start us in the right direction, there must be an active learning. This is especially true with this virtue of hospitality. It is a practical virtue demanding practical skills. Yet, in learning some simple skills, we can accomplish our goal: doing for others and making them feel loved. When we see hospitality as a virtue and not just something we do everyday, we bring supernatural insight into the practice of skills we do daily as mothers. This is what we want to give our girls: the knowledge of how to do these skills well but also, the spiritual foundation of why we do them.

This program is designed to help our girls understand this and to teach our "little women" the practical skills of hospitality they will use throughout their lives. They will learn how to cook, how to set a table, how to clear a table, how to clean a room properly, how to prepare a room for a guest, how to make a bed properly, how to sew, how to appreciate good literature...and many other things. Mother Teresa said once, "We must not do great things but little things with great love." She herself was a proof that we don't need much, but we do need a plan, love, and the knowledge of how to execute it.

When I was in grade school, I remember my mom warned me, that if I chose to make my bed poorly one more time, I would have to make it perfect ten times in a row. My mom was, and is, a most gentle woman. She was never one to scold harshly, or one to set out ultimatums such as this. Maybe that's why the following day has been left in my memory as a good example to do my work well, whatever it may be. For, the very next day, I made my bed sloppily as usual and went to school. This particular day, I had a birthday party to attend after school. The end of the day came, and I was all ready to go to my friend's party when I heard my sister call to me. "Mom said you have to come home now to take care of something. You will have to join the others a little later."

Sure enough, my mom was waiting for me in my room with my covers removed from my bed. "OK honey, let's make your bed." So I made it with tight covers, pillow perfectly tucked, and thought I was done. I did my best smoothing and tucking, as I really knew how, I just never took the time. This time it looked perfect.

"Good job," my mom said. Off came all the covers. It was then I knew she was serious. Nine more times my perfectly made covers met the floor. Upon the last tuck of my tenth turn, my mom said, "Now you'll remember to do a good job." And I did. Give it your all and your goal will happen.

Skills may be essential to this virtue, but a proper attitude or giving your best is equally important. Our "little women" will learn to do these skills well, because they will come to see through this program, that the learned skills are just a means to the end of serving others out of love.

Each month the program is broken into a particular skill related to hospitality. The class begins with a spiritual story, from the Bible or from a saint's life, told in a particular way to inspire the girls to practice the skill of the day. This is followed by an example and passage from classic literature. Louisa May Alcott is a perfect author to illustrate this for you. She showed hospitality as a virtue so beautifully through out many of her works. These passages give the girls a concrete example to discuss, relate to, and simply enjoy. Following this discussion, the hands-on lesson begins. The hostess gives a demonstration of the skill in a prepared area of her home. The girls are then invited to practice the skill in a fun way, play a related game, or sometimes even role play. Cooking, for example, involves the girls making cookies, as a way to practice measuring and following a recipe.

Lastly, there is recommended literature for the girls, field trips to go on, and a

12

"Take Home" page in their companion book with several suggested activities to practice that month. These pages will also contain important notes or reminders from the meeting, so the girls can remember how to practice the skills they learned. Just because they learned the skill once, doesn't mean they'll remember all the parts. The Take Home will help them to do this, as it repeats things from the lessons when necessary. For instance, it includes a copy of a proper place setting if the girls forget where things are to be placed on the table. Please go over these items with girls after coming home from the meeting so they may plan and choose which things they want to do that month. The Take Homes also contain formats to follow as in the class on correspondence. That month has sample letters and forms for all different occasions to write. At the beginning of the companion book will be a calendar of the skills taught each month and what the girls will need to bring. Refer to this each month so your girls will always be prepared. This calendar will help you plan ahead for materials and will also show the order of the program. This book can be kept in a 3-ring binder, a "hospitality binder," with a copy of the program cover placed in the front pocket. The binder can be filled with section dividers labeled for each skill and filled with page protectors and photo pages so the girls can add their own findings. It will become the girls own resource for their skills, as they grow from our Little Women into Women raising their own.

Our Lord and Lady spent their lives in the service of others. In so doing, they were showing us what a perfect man and a perfect woman should be like. God did not intend us to live for ourselves. The first act of doing for ourselves is, and was, called "original sin." If Eve had been a helpmate to Adam, as God intended her to be, she would have strengthened him. It was in turning to her own needs and desires that God's plan was not fulfilled.

Hospitality is a fun virtue for us to practice and an easy path to heaven, if we learn to form the habit of thinking of others before ourselves. In so doing, we will be living our lives in the service of others and finding our own joy along the journey. Happy travels and may God bless you!

Jubilee Prayer for Home

In 2000 when the Jubilee year was celebrated, there was a blessing and opening of the great door in St. Peter's in Rome. In imitation of this, families across the world blessed the doors to their own homes and used this prayer as a consecration. It is shared here with you that you might say it with your daughters as you bless your home as a family, with the petition for hospitality, for your home and your family. Simply make a cross on your door with holy water as you all say this prayer:

Blessed are you, O Lord our God,
For you guide our footsteps.
You bless our coming in and our going out,
From birth until death, you hold us in your care.

Bless this door, O Lord,
Which we consecrate to this time of preparation.
Each day we pass this place,
Draw us more deeply into your presence
And the wonders of your love for us.

You are the door to the Kingdom of God,
The sheep gate to life eternal,
O portal of eternal peace, our new and living way,
Loose our sins and open for us the door to salvation.

O God, protect our going out and our coming in;
Let us share the hospitality of this home with all who visit us.
May the poor find rest within these walls and
All who hunger find refreshment in our home.

Lead us home through you, to you, and with you, one God, forever and ever. Amen.

Letter to the Hostess:

In this course, our little women are learning the skill and virtue of hospitality. Many think hospitality is merely throwing a party and welcoming others into your home. Although this is a way to practice the virtue, this is a more secular view of the word. There is a good in welcoming others, but the true virtue comes from the foundation of doing for others because of our Faith. Our Lord and Lady continually opened their hearts, conversations, skill and friendship to others. This is a great example to us. Our call to join the Kingdom of Heaven is the virtue of hospitality in its perfect state. Our Lord is welcoming us into His home, forever.

This is why we are each called to serve one another; to be aware that others have needs, and try to find the best way to satisfy those. Many times, this is a very fun thing to do. It brings us joy when we entertain or make others happy. Other times, we serve, when we do not want to, but do, because we should. Either way, we need to know how to serve. This is a practical virtue. This program is designed to equip its participants with the skills necessary to practice the virtue of hospitality in everyday ways, as well as in formal settings. Something as simple as a smile, or little note, can be a form of hospitality, but can extend to having someone into your home as a guest. In this course, the girls are taught how to meet the needs of others in their homes and outside their homes, how to include others and how to be gracious guests. "We know not the time, nor the hour." (cf Matthew 24:36) We must know how to be hospitable, as Abraham did, when he was serving the angels he thought to be strangers.

The path of hospitality is the path to serving others. It is a way to make everyone we meet feel special.

The virtue of hospitality is a disposition by which, we open our homes and hearts to others, to foster friendship and to share in each other's interests, while also serving those in need.

The skill of hospitality is the practice of order and art in different areas of our home, which can also be extended to others in their homes.

Let us begin by thanking you for your hospitality in teaching these little women. You will have fun and be rewarded as you see these girls joyfully learning the skills you are teaching them. Enjoy it! Virtue is not all pain and sacrifice; this one is lots of fun.

The format page explains the structure for each class in this course. First, there is a holy inspiration, a way for the girls to see the skill they are about to learn, rooted in the virtue of hospitality. Next, a passage from literature highlights the skill, bringing a light heart to its practice. Following the reading, the girls will discuss the passage. Finally, the lesson is taught. You will prepare the room ahead of time and enter it for the demonstration part of the skill.

You will want to read through the entire lesson first, to become familiar with the whole, before worrying too much about the parts. Then, go back and see what you will need, which is indicated in the "Notes to the Hostess" and "Things Hostess Needs." Plan for these. Feel free to write or make notes on your copy given to you to teach the class. If you have any questions, call the coordinator for this program. Ask the Holy Spirit to guide you in your words and your preparation. He always surprises us! Also, talk to the guardian angels of the girls you are teaching. They will tell you what each girl needs.

Lastly, the girls each have a hospitality book for themselves. Each month there is a special "Take Home" page, as it is called, that gives them ideas and ways to practice their skills. At the conclusion of the meeting, make sure to go over the page with the girls for the skill you are teaching. The girls will keep this book in a binder and hopefully add their own findings to this binder as they grow.

The skill you are asked to teach is laid out in detail. If you have a creative idea to implement, that is your privilege as hostess, as long as it sticks to the general guidelines for teaching the skill of the month. Make sure and notice the time parameters for each section so you don't run out of time. In this format, time can go quickly, so make sure to have control of the discussions, questions, and practices. Don't let the girls get too far on tangents in their discussions. The beauty of having different moms teach the class is the individuality that each mom can bring. We all have our strengths, and, hopefully, we all pick a skill to teach that is in line with this.

Lastly, if you have something that you want to give the girls, this would only make the program richer. If you have a favorite recipe or tip for the skill you are doing, have it on index cards or copies on paper or cardstock for each girl to put in their binder. What a lovely addition for them as they grow to have these personal touches from all the moms that taught them how to become a true "little woman." Sign the card and date it, so they remember who it came from, in the years to come.

FIELD TRIPS Each month has optional field trips. If you are someone that likes to plan outings, these are some fun suggestions and spiritual works of mercy that you can organize for your group related to the skill you just taught. It is up to you to organize and inform others of the field trip. If it is easiest, make flyers and send them home at the meeting.

Format for each Lesson- 2 hours (including snack)

Time to Begin: Sit in a comfortable area for prayers and book discussion, away from the area that has been set up for the practical part of the lesson.

Opening Prayer: Welcome girls and begin with this prayer, our motto. 5 minutes

Lord, make me an instrument of your peace.
Where there is hatred, let me sow love
Where there is injury, pardon
Where there is doubt, faith
Where there is despair, hope
Where there is darkness, light
Where there is sadness, joy
Divine Master,
Grant that I may not so much seek
To be consoled, as to console
To be understood, as to understand
To be loved, as to love
For it is in giving that we receive,
It is in pardoning, that we are pardoned,
It is in dying that we are born to eternal life.

Holy Inspiration: Read to girls. 5 minutes

Read Literature Section and Discussion: 15 minutes

Assemble for Lesson in designated place: Please remind the girls to be courteous to each other as they proceed in, no running!

Hostess: Explain the skill as part of hospitality and demonstrate the skill. 10-15 minutes.

Practice Skill: Follow directions for this section. Time will vary, about one hour

Conclusion: Do any other directions in particular lesson. Read through Take Home with girls if time allows. Encourage them to get together and have fun with the ideas in this sheet so they can make the skill a habit. Inform the girls of any materials they will need for the next meeting.

Closing Prayer: Give thanks to all the saints and holy women who have helped us today. May we all grow ourselves into holy, little women.

Snack: 15 minutes if time allows

Departure

Opening Prayer to St. Francis

Lord, make me an instrument of your peace.
Where there is hatred, let me sow love
Where there is injury, pardon
Where there is doubt, faith
Where there is despair, hope
Where there is darkness, light
Where there is sadness, joy
Divine Master,
Grant that I may not so much seek
To be consoled, as to console
To be understood, as to understand
To be loved, as to love
For it is in giving that we receive,
It is in pardoning, that we are pardoned,
It is in dying that we are born to eternal life.

Calendar of Supplies Girls Need to Bring

1. **September - Cooking -** The girls will be learning the basics of cooking and preparing a recipe.

2. **October - How to Clean a Room -** The girls will learn the proper way to dust, sweep, vacuum and tidy a room.

3. **November - How to Set and Clear a Table -** The girls will learn the proper way to set and clear a formal table.

4. **December - Table Manners and Conversation -** The girls will practice their manners at the table and do role plays of how to treat and talk with others.

5. **January - Preparing a Room for a Guest -** The girls will employ their cleaning skills and learn to make a bed properly with square corners. They will learn to fold sheets, fold towels, and learn what should and shouldn't be in a room for a guest.

6. **February - Correspondence -** Bring name and address of someone you want to write. The girls will learn the proper way to write for many occasions. They will learn to talk on paper.

7. **March - Bringing Hospitality to Others/ Being a Good Guest -** The girls will learn and discuss the many ways they can practice the virtue of hospitality away from home. They will come to understand what situations require this virtue from them, and how they can best serve others' needs. There are some wonderful stories to share in their Take Home page this month.

8. ***April - Sewing and Dressing Modestly -** Bring material for their hospitality apron that they will be making this month. You will need scissors and thread to match. Material: two pieces of fabric measuring 32 x 20 inches. You can choose a plain broadcloth for the backside or another print for a two-sided apron. You need thick ribbon that doesn't unravel for ties. You need two 24 inch ribbons and two 15 inch ribbons. These will be your tie at the neck and waist.

9. **May - How to Plan and Prepare for a Party - Mother's Day Tea -** This is two parts. The meeting itself will be the planning and a week or so later, will be the tea party. **For the Tea Party:** Bring prepared recipes, your apron, guest page, and your mom's favorite tea cup. The girls will be serving their guests, their moms.

10. **June - Book Club - Eight Cousins by Louisa May Alcott -** Please read this ahead and bring your copy with your name in it, or place an index card in it with your name if it is from the library. You will be discussing this book at the meeting. This will be followed by a social hour.

Hospitality: The Skill of Cooking: How to Measure and Follow a Recipe

"Blessed are those who are invited to the wedding supper of the Lamb." Revelations 19:9

Holy Inspiration: The Benedictine Order is an order that strives to welcome others through their hospitality and generosity. They are always gracious hosts to those in need, feeding them and giving shelter. St. Benedict, in his "Rule" for the order, stresses the importance that we must accept people the way they are, and to see Christ in them. We grow closer to Our Lord and Our Lady by living alongside people who aren't perfect, and need our kind acts of hospitality. The Benedictine Rule calls its followers to accept everyone who comes to their door. They may be poor, a traveler of a different religion or race. Anyone should be received as if they were Christ.

There was a particular order in Massachusetts that would host a Saturday night gathering for youth. They would fill a table with sweets and sodas for each child. Then all were invited to a big screen showing of a classic movie. It was a wonderful way, in this modern world, to bring the tradition from St. Benedict to those who could not know him.

The gesture was simple but very welcoming. Moreover, it created an atmosphere where the youth could foster friendship among themselves. Friendship is the easiest way to extend ourselves to others by listening to, sharing, enjoying, and being truly kind to one another. Including others, especially those that are shy or alone, is one of the best ways that each of us can bring St. Benedict's lessons to a modern world.

Our Lady's Patronage: It seems appropriate to put the skill of cooking under the patronage of Our Lady of the Eucharist. This lovely image of Mary adoring Christ in the Eucharist is a tremendous reminder of how Christ feeds us everytime we receive Him in the Blessed Sacrament. As devotion to Mary can only lead to deeper knowledge and friendship with Christ, we keep in mind as we feed others how Christ nourishes our souls through His Body, Blood, Soul and Divinity.

Charm: Cookie Jar

Literature Example: In *Little Men* by Louisa May Alcott, the chapter entitled "Pattypans" explains how a young girl named Daisy needs something to occupy her time. She is surrounded by boys, so Aunt Jo designs a pretend play made just for Daisy, since she loves to cook but doesn't have a place to do it.

> 'It's all ready, come on,' and, tucking Ted under her arm....Aunt Jo promptly led the way upstairs.
> 'I don't see anything,' said Daisy...

'Do you hear anything?' asked Aunt Jo....

Daisy did hear an odd crackling, and then a purry little sound as of a kettle singing. These noises came from behind a curtain drawn before a deep bay window. Daisy snatched it back, gave one joyful 'Oh!' and then stood gazing with delight at- what do you think?

A wide seat ran round the three sides of the window; on one side hung and stood all sorts of little pots and pans, tea set, and on the middle part a cooking stove. Not a tin one, that was of no use, but a real iron stove, big enough to cook for a large family of very hungry dolls. But the best of it was that a real fire burned in it, real steam came out of the nose of the little teakettle and the lid of the little boiler actually danced a jig, the water inside bubbled so hard. A pane of glass had been taken out and replaced by a sheet of tin, with a hole for the small funnel, and real smoke went sailing away outside so naturally that it did one's heart good to see it. The box of wood with a hod of charcoal stood nearby; just above hung dustpan, brush, and broom; a little market basket was on the low table at which Daisy used to play, and over the back of her little chair hung a white apron with a bib, and a droll mobcap. The sun shone in as if she enjoyed the fun, the little stove roared beautifully, the kettle steamed, the new tins sparkled on the walls, the pretty china stood in tempting rows and it was altogether as cheery and complete a kitchen as any child could desire.

Daisy stood quite still after the first glad 'Oh!' but her eyes went quickly from one charming object to another, brightening as they looked, till they came to Aunt Jo's merry face; there they stopped as the happy little girl hugged her, saying gratefully.

'Oh, aunty, it's a splendid new play! Can I really cook at the dear stove, and have parties and mess, and sweep, and make fires that truly burn? I like it so much! What made you think of it?'

'Your liking to make gingersnaps with Asia made me think of it,' said Mrs. Bhaer.......'I knew Asia wouldn't let you mess in her kitchen very often, and it wouldn't be safe at this fire up here, so I thought I'd see if I could find a little stove for you, and teach you how to cook; that would be fun, and useful too. So I traveled round among the toy shops, but everything large cost too much and I was thinking I should have to give it up, when I met Uncle Teddy. As soon as he knew what I was about, he said he wanted to help....He teased me about my cooking when we were young, and said I must teach Bess as well as you, and went on buying all sorts of nice little things for my 'cooking class', as he called it.'

....'You must study hard and learn to make all kinds of things for he says he shall come out to tea very often, and expects something uncommonly nice.'

'It's the sweetest, dearest kitchen in the world, and I'd rather study with it than do anything else. Can't I learn pies, and cake, and macaroni, and everything?' cried Daisy, dancing round the room with a new saucepan in one hand and the tiny poker in the other.

'All in good time. This is to be a useful play, I am to help you, and you are to be my cook, so I shall tell you what to do, and show you how. Then we shall have things fit to eat, and you will be really learning how to cook on a small scale. ...'

'...What shall I do first?' asked Sally....

'First of all, put on this clean cap and apron. I am rather old-fashioned, and I like my cook to be very tidy.'..."

Discussion: This chapter from *Little Men* sets a nice stage for the program and learning to cook. As you ask the girls what they think of the passage, guide the conversation to notice the following: It teaches that steps must be taken to prepare a kitchen with the proper tools and equipment. Then there must be a plan for the meal, and the shopping for the necessary ingredients. Most of all, a new cook must listen well, and learn from someone who knows how. First, there must be kitchen safety as Jo points out. Daisy could not cook on any stove but one that is safe and suited for her needs. Next, a cook must be neat and tidy. Cooking involves order as well as creativity. An apron and careful measuring can lend itself to a tidier kitchen while the delectable treats or savory morsels are cooking.

Notice how well behaved Daisy is as she listens to Aunt Jo's directions. Even in her excitement, she does not forget to be thankful. This is so important when someone does something nice for us.

Discuss uses for this skill: Cooking is a primary way to show hospitality to others, and can be a corporal work of mercy. (Ask girls to think of ways cooking can show hospitality to others in this way. Make notes that can be saved by girls for their binders if they so choose.)

Be sure to mention the following if the girls did not think of them before beginning the practical part of the lesson. Cooking can be used to:

1. **Help at home in the kitchen**
2. **Prepare for friends to come for a visit**
3. **Bring a meal to someone in need: someone sick or a mom who just had a baby**
4. **Bring a meal to a priest or someone living alone**
5. **Use this skill to make presents**
6. **Use to host a bake sale as a fundraiser for a good cause**
7. **Just for fun! Cook together for pleasure is a way to enjoy each other**
8. **Make breakfast in bed for a family member on a special day like their birthday**

The Lesson

Note to Hostess: Check the list below in the "Demonstration" part to be certain you have all the items collected. The kitchen is a fun place for girls, so try to interact while you teach the lesson. When you measure flour, for instance, as an example of measuring dry ingredients, have the girls come up and practice measuring one by one to make sure they level off or completely fill their measuring cup. In baking, precision is important. (I once had a friend who substituted baking soda for some of the flour because she didn't have enough flour. She didn't understand that precision in baking is necessary or your recipe will not turn out. Savory dishes do not require as much precision but in baking it is essential. Needless to say, the cookies didn't turn out.) For this class, based on the number of girls, try to make one or two extra recipes, before the girls arrive so they will have some to take home.

In the practice section, note the things that you need to set up for the girls. There will be a station for each girl at a long kitchen table or counter for them to measure, crack, separate and whisk eggs.

Things Hostess needs: The basics indicated in demonstration such as measuring spoons and cups, plus 2 bowls for each of the girls to practice measuring flour and cracking eggs. It would be a good idea to buy a package of paper bowls for this exercise, for easy disposal. Warehouse clubs are great places to get these inexpensively as well as bulk eggs and flour, for the practice part. Provide extra eggs or ask another mom to bring some. Cracking and separating eggs is a primary skill in both baking and savory cooking, so you want to let the girls have a lot of practice. (If it is too difficult to get extras of things, send an email to the girls before the meeting, and ask them to bring a baggy of flour and bowl for the class.) Have a general bowl of flour or other dry ingredient of choice at each end of the table for the girls to use for measuring practice. Have cup and spoon measuring implements and butter knives. Whisks can be used if adding that practice. (Forks also make good whisks.) Lastly, paper plates or little baggies for girls to bring treats home in. You will also need the ingredients for the recipe, or have the girls bring some of them, if you choose.

* It would be nice if you want to make a copy of your favorite recipe for each girl to put in their binder.

Demonstration:

1. Show measuring spoons and cups. You might also show the beginning of a cookbook which shows all measurements and conversions.

2. Show how to measure wet and dry ingredients (use back of knife to level off) Talk about different terms for wet vs. dry ingredients like liters. Pints are for liquid

and cups are for both.

3. Show how to crack an egg and how to separate whites from yolks. Crack on the side of a bowl or on the counter itself, and put two thumbs at crack and pull apart. (Either use the shells themselves to separate white from yolk or crack egg into bowl and simply grab out the yolk. This last method is fun and really hands on.) Demonstrate whisking at this point as well with wire whisk or fork. Poke the yolks first as it makes it much faster to whisk and make sure the girls see that the white needs to be completely whisked with the yolk..

4. Show stove safety. Always put handles away from the flame and have hot pads nearby. Never reach over an open flame. When cooking with oil or anything else that can flare up, teach the girls that flour is an easy extinguisher. Flour works great on oil spills on the floor or anywhere since it absorbs the oil and makes it easier to clean up. (I have hands on experience when my five gallon container of vegetable oil spilled on my kitchen floor. Flour saved the day.) Another item to remind the girls about stove safety is to emphasize that pot handles should always face away from the flame and turned to the side or back of the oven so that little hands cannot pull hot pots down upon themselves.

5. Show mixer safety. Never put your hands near the beaters when it's on. Always check that the mixer is off before plugging it in. Turn the mixer off before adding the next ingredient, as it is so easy to have the spoon get caught up in the beaters.

6. Show how to prepare for a recipe: lay all ingredients out next to the measuring cups. As they are used, put them away.

7. Clean up as you go. It is much easier to clean a pan or bowl and reuse it during your recipe, than to pile up a bunch of pans.

Practice: Ask another mom to help supervise as it will be difficult to watch too many girls cracking and measuring, if you have lots of girls in your group.

1. Have each girl stand in place over her bowl, and have them practice cracking and separating at least two eggs. Do as many eggs as you are willing to provide.

2. An added practice skill could be whisking, depending on time. The girls will probably have to share whisks. Tell them to be patient and watch each other. (Of course, they can use forks.)

3. Have each girl practice measuring a dry ingredient such as sugar or flour, with

both a cup, or fraction thereof, and a measuring spoon. Provide a butter knife for leveling off. You may want to provide a separate bowl for this, so you can reuse the flour.

Using preferably hand mixers but can use standing mixer: Instructor may choose a different recipe if she prefers to, but try to make it something that will cook while the girls are still there to enjoy their work. Perhaps, make extra recipes ahead of time, so the girls can bring some home to their families. Prepare with little paper plates and plastic wrap that they can use to take their treats home. You want them to be proud of their new skill and be able to share it with their family.

Note: Teach the girls to always read through the entire recipe first, so they understand the order in which it should be put together.

Make Cookies: Russian Tea Surprise Cookies

Break girls into groups to help make the different parts of the recipe. All can roll cookies around kisses. (You may need extra kisses for those that stray into hungry girls' mouths.) Explain to the girls that many cookie recipes call for creaming the butter and the sugar. It is important to do this well to attain the right consistency in the final cookie. Also, tell the girls to always make their cookies uniform in size when baking. Otherwise, some will be too small and burn and others, too large and be undercooked.

In this recipe, there is a natural size for all the cookies because of the kiss.

1 cup butter
2 ¼ cups all purpose flour
1/3 cup sugar
1 tsp vanilla
1 cup chopped pecans (make sure no one has a nut allergy)
½ bag chocolate kisses or more
1 cup sifted powdered sugar

Preheat oven to 325 degrees. In a mixing bowl beat butter for 30 seconds. Add half of the flour, the sugar and 1 tablespoon of water and the vanilla. Beat until thoroughly combined. Beat in remaining flour. Stir in pecans (can be left out if someone has a nut allergy). Unwrap chocolate kisses and take a tablespoon or so of dough, and form around chocolate kiss to form a ball. NO PART OF KISSES SHOULD SHOW. Place on ungreased cookie sheet and bake for about 20 minutes until bottoms are slightly browned. Check cookies at 15 minutes to see how they are cooking. Ovens vary and you don't want to burn the cookies. Cool cookies on wire rack . Gently shake to coat cooled cookies in bag filled with the cup of powdered sugar, use more if necessary. Makes about 30 cookies.

Option 2: Surprise Meringue Kisses

This is a good option to use up the separated egg whites. Egg whites are sometimes tricky to work with, so supervision by an experienced cook will be required. You will need a hand mixer to stiffen the egg whites. Also make sure your whites have no yolks in them at all or they won't stiffen correctly. Use a deep, narrow bowl for stiffening. Let the eggs come to room temperature before mixing for best results.

3 egg whites
1 tsp vanilla
1/4 tsp cream of tartar (in spice section)
1/4 tsp peppermint extract
dash salt
1 cup granulated sugar
1/2 bag chocolate kisses or more
green colored sugar

Beat egg whites, vanilla and cream of tartar in bowl. When soft peaks form (after about a minute) gradually add sugar and continue beating. Beat until very stiff peaks form. Drop by tablespoons on slightly greased cookie sheet about 1 1/2 inches apart. Press a chocolate kiss into each cookie. With spatula, bring meringue up and over candy and swirl the top. Sprinkle with the sugar. Bake at 275 degrees for 30 minutes. Cool on rack.

Conclusion: Ask the girls if they have any questions about the kitchen or how to prepare a recipe. Have girls make plates of cookies, and wrap to take home. Put a sticker on each plate, with name of each girl, so they don't forget it. Give each girl a copy of your favorite recipe with a note from you, and date it, to put into their binders under the cooking skill section. Tell the girls they can bring copies of their favorite recipe next month to share with everyone in the group. End the session with a prayer to St. Benedict, asking for his guidance as the girls begin their journey on the road to serving others.

Take Home

Do one or more of the list below. Make a note of what you did or write a paragraph to put into your hospitality binder under this skill.

Uses for this skill: Cooking is a primary way to show hospitality to others, and can be a corporal work of mercy.

1. Use to help at home in the kitchen
2. Prepare for friends to come for a visit
3. Bring a meal to someone in need: someone sick or a mom who just had a baby
4. Bring a meal to a priest or someone living alone
5. Use this skill to make presents
6. Use to host a bake sale, as a fundraiser for a good cause
7. Just for fun! Cook together for pleasure as a way to enjoy each other
8. Make breakfast in bed for a family member on a special day like their birthday
9. Send a note with your favorite recipe to someone who might enjoy it.

Note: If you have a favorite recipe, make some copies for the girls in your group and begin a recipe exchange next month. Print it and glue it to 3x5 or 4x6 index cards. These will fit great into photo pages that can be added to your binder.

Field Trip Options:

*   Visit a soup kitchen run by the Sisters of Charity or other Catholic organization. See how others use their cooking to be hospitable to the poor and homeless.

*   Donate food to a food pantry.

*   Volunteer to do a 'Meals on Wheels Program' - through your parish or community.

*   Make a schedule for a priest or someone in need, and call others in your hospitality group to volunteer for a day to bring a meal. Families who have a child who is seriously sick would appreciate this so much. Then, make a card and put everyone's name on it, with the schedule. This way the receiver will know what days to expect a prepared meal. Make sure you check for food allergies before preparing a meal for someone else.

*   Volunteer to help at a parish pancake breakfast or bake sale. Either bring an item to donate or serve at it yourself, or both. Or organize a bake sale as a fund raiser for a good cause, or something your parish may be in need of.

Recommended Reading: *Little Men* by Louisa May Alcott. Audio book also available.

Recipe **TAKE HOME**

Begin your own collection of recipes to keep in this section of your hospitality binder with the recipe on pages 22 and 23.

FURTHER RECIPES: Use cardstock and attach other recipes, using recipe or index cards and a glue stick . Then slide into page. Or buy photo pages to slide the recipe cards into. Decorate pages with stamps or stickers.

Hospitality: The Skill of Dusting and Cleaning a Room Properly

"Come to me, all you who labor and are burdened, and I will give you rest. For my yolk is easy, and my burden is light." (Mt 11:28-30)

Holy Inspiration: During World War II, there were two girls from Poland, probably in their teens, who were hiding some Jews from the Nazis, who wanted to take them prisoners. These girls were Catholic and had been taught well. They were also very courageous. They had heard that the Nazis were in the neighborhood checking for hidden Jews and they began to panic. "What shall we do?" they thought. They could not give up the lives of these innocent people that they were protecting. So the older sister said, "when they come, we will do what we do best: clean." And this is what they did. The soldiers came and the girls went about their dusting and their cleaning as if nothing unusual was going on. The soldiers never found the innocent Jews which the girls had hidden beneath the floor. This is a beautiful and heroic example to others how a well-learned skill can be used to serve. Although most of us will never be called to this level of heroism, we can still use our skills for those in need. We can especially serve our family with this skill when we perform our tasks with a joyful disposition. Remember that we may perform a task well, but if we do it with a bad attitude, there is no virtue.

Our Lady's Patronage: We place this skill under the patronage of the Immaculate Heart of Mary. Our Lady's was conceived and born without any original sin, thus God made her soul clean from its inception. The image of the Immaculate Heart is a comforting and inspirational ideal. Like Christs' heart, it burns for love of us. Many of us may not like to clean, but if we keep in mind the happy holy family in Nazareth, where the pure heart of Mary cleaned for her family with virtue and joy, we can rely on her to help us do the same.

Charm: Button

Literature Example: There is a wonderful chapter in a book called *All of a Kind Family* by Sydney Taylor entitled: "Dusting is Fun." The girls hated to dust and clean the front room, a job they often had to do. Listen to what happened when the mother in the story devises a game that would incite her reluctant girls to do a better job in their dusting.

She decided to hide twelve buttons in the dining room, the designated room to be cleaned. The girls each took a turn cleaning this room each week, but one daughter, Sarah, in particular, was the greatest at excuses to try and get out of the loathsome chore. Ironically, once mother announced this new game, Sarah, the least likely to volunteer and most apt to do a poor job, proclaimed with great delight that it was her day to clean the room. She grabbed the duster and embraced the challenge to find all dozen buttons that her mother so carefully hid. If Sarah found all twelve buttons, her mother knew she had done a thorough cleaning job. If, on the other hand, she did not find all twelve, she missed cleaning a place she should have.

First off, Sarah cleaned the dining room table, the most obvious place and found a button once she moved a few pieces on top to be dusted. Then she cleaned the legs of the table, the hard to clean chairs and the piano. Having succeeded in uncovering a few buttons, she was motivated to continue to the more daunting places, namely, the inside of the piano, the baseboards around the room, the molding and the window ledges. Each time she was rewarded for her diligence. Even when she almost skipped something, she persevered and discovered more treasures. She lifted doilies, did the piano foot pedals, picked up shells and dusted those and any other knick-knacks around the room. To her satisfaction, Sarah found all dozen buttons her mother had hidden. To her mother's approval, a well-dusted room was the result of this adventure and hopefully, the beginning of a good habit for all her girls.

Discussion: How did the girls like this story? Do the girls in this class clean this thoroughly? What are items mentioned, that they would have never thought of cleaning? What do you think about doing a job well? When cleaning a room, we can make it fun if we try to do it with our best effort. This is where the love and the joy of the virtue come into this skill. We must give our all when we clean, and remember that even when we clean alone, we are still serving the others that will enjoy the room later.

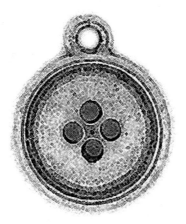

The Lesson

Notes to the Hostess: The hostess should prepare a room to dust and clean for this lesson, aside from the place you will gather in for the literature segments. This is probably the only time in your life that you will be told to let the dust gather for guests, but it is very important to have a dusty room for the girls to practice cleaning. Hide twelve buttons or even chocolate coins for fun before the girls come, in the area to be cleaned. Have ten or more items out of place for the girls to pick up. Put books out on the table, toys on the floor such as blocks, legos, etc. Then, have a basket or box in which they belong nearby. Maybe put a sweater on the couch and shoes on the floor, typical items dropped in a home. Remember, try not to dust for a week or more in this room, so there will be plenty of dusting practice for the girls.

Things the Hostess Needs: This lesson does not require many extras. It is more about how you prepare for it than what you prepare. Have 12 buttons or chocolate coins or pennies as mentioned above, a duster and dusting cloth moist for wiping, broom and dustpan, vacuum, pencils and paper for additional game.

Demonstration: Show the girls the following, cleaning only one item, as an example. (Do not clean the whole room in your demonstration or there will be nothing left for them to practice.)

* Straightening is the first thing to bring order to the room before one can begin to clean.

* Dusting is always the first thing in cleaning, so use the literature passage as a guide to teach the girls how and what to dust. The literature passage is almost a manual on how to dust.

* Remove all items from shelves, tables, piano, etc. Dust the items themselves, and the surface, before replacing them. Teach them how to dust a lamp, top, shade, middle and bottom. Teach them to dust any nooks and crannies in a table or chair with cut-work in the wood. Teach them to dust woodwork on walls, doors and backs of chairs. Teach them to dust items on walls such as frames or sconces. Don't forget the chandeliers. Even if you do not have these items, please tell the girls to do them if they were in a room. Every room is unique in its contents but uniform in its procedure to clean.

* If you are so unfortunate as to have eight-legged friends living in your home, remind the girls to check for cobwebs around the corners of the room near the ceiling and on chandeliers. They are also popular under furniture and above bookcases.

* After dusting and straightening is complete, depending on the room, decide what is next. It may be vacuuming, sweeping, etc. If vacuuming, teach the girls to make nice lines, not all over the place, and to do edges well. Tell them to take the time to use the hand tools on a vacuum for edges or under furniture where the vacuum can't reach. If sweeping, teach girls to sweep under furniture and along edges of room. No sweeping the pile under the carpet! Use a dustpan. Lastly, make sure all pillows are straight and neat on the couches or chairs. Make certain all throw blankets are neatly folded and you're done. Voila, beautiful room!

Practice: Have girls repeat your actions, taking turns, for dusting, straightening, vacuuming, etc. Of course, the dust will actually be gone before all the girls are done practicing. Still continue as if it was there. The girls should practice removing objects, dusting the objects themselves, picture frames, lamps, etc. from top to bottom. Dust the surface and replace the objects. Continue with straightening, periodically dumping and messing up for the next girl. I'm sure you'll have lots of volunteers for that. Watch them vacuum and sweep to see that they understand and remember to do the edges and under furniture.

Extra Activity: *items needed: paper & pencils - You should have enough to fill your time but if you need an added game, have the girls study the room in order so they know where everything belongs. Then have everyone close their eyes, no peeking, and remove several items from the room. Have the girls each write down all the things you removed, if they can remember. It sharpens their observation skills for details in a room, and is a whole lot of fun. You can also play this game with a tray of things, 15 or so. Show the tray, let them study the things and remove an item. They can write down what was missing. Alternately, let them study the tray and then take the entire tray away. Have them write as many of the 15 things they can remember on the tray. The winner has the most correct items.

Conclusion: When all the girls have cleaned and practiced, remind them about doing a job well. It is easy and fast to dust the surface and vacuum or sweep the middle, but when asked to do a job, or volunteering to do one to help someone, always give it your best. There was a cook I read about who was serving a party for 200 people. One of his helpers brought him some potatoes that didn't taste very good. The cook answered, "No good, I can't serve this, my name is going on it." Well, your name is going on any work you do and God sees it. It is easier to do a good job when you know it is for someone else, because you want them to have the best.

Take Home:

* Try this system out at home. Ask each girl to clean a family or living room and have their mom see how they did. Happy Cleaning!

* Teach a younger sibling how to clean well using the hidden buttons game. Remember to be kind in teaching. If you are impatient with your sibling because they don't do it right, then you are not being a good teacher. Teaching others our skills is another way to help them but we must be patient.

* Help a family you know who just moved into a new house. There is lots of unpacking to do, and lots of cleaning when the unpacking is done. See if you can help out.

* Gather some friends to volunteer to clean a new mom's house. It's hard to get everything done when you just have a baby. What a nice baby present this would be.

* Volunteer to clean your church.

* Clean up and have some friends over for a movie and popcorn. Invite a friend you think may not usually be included.

Recommended Reading: *All of a Kind Family* by Sydney Taylor

Recommended Movies: *Cheaper by the Dozen* (with Jeanne Crain, Myrna Loy and Clifton Web), and it's sequel, *Belles on Their Toes*, about the true life, Gilbreth family. The Gilbreths had 12 children and were efficiency experts. This produces many funny, time-saving techniques for everyday life. In *Cheaper by the Dozen*, there is a scene in which the children must allot the work because there is not enough money to hire extra help. They kind of moan and groan but then get the work done. The second movie, *Belles on Their Toes*, practically opens with a scene of all the kids pitching in to clean, inside and out, from top to bottom, while singing "I Want to be Lazy". Music is always a great way to bring life to your cleaning. Both these movies are based on the books by Frank and Ernestine Gilbreth, two of the older children.

Talk a little about how a table setting is like a well wrapped package, even if the gift itself is not huge, the wrapping is memorable. Some people may not be great cooks but can still have a simple meal well presented, making the guest feel very special.

The Lesson

Notes to Hostess: You may want to look up table settings in a good etiquette book like Emily Post, Amy Vanderbilt or Miss Manners to brush up your own knowledge of formal table setting. Any library would have a copy to look at and use as a reference.

1. Have a copy of *The Harvey Girls* set to the scene near the beginning, right after they get off the train and are all going into the Harvey House. The scene is actually a song in which they teach the girls how to prepare their uniforms and the tables. Judy Garland is in uniform. "The Harvey system, I must say, primarily pertains to perfection in the way we meet the train, perfection in the dining room, perfection in the Harvey uniform...." NOTE: If you can't find the movie, give the lesson without. Do read the history of the Harvey Girls, perhaps have a picture from the internet to show the girls what a Harvey girl looked like.

2. Look at demonstration to prepare what you will need.

3. Write out a sample menu for the girls to view. It must have all the courses of a formal dinner for the girls to be able to put out the various utensils and dishes of such a meal (bread, soup, salad, entrée, dessert, wine/champagne, coffee). The menu is a reference in setting the table. I suggest using paper bowls, small dessert plates for butter plates, salad plates and dinner plates. Paper may be easier so your good dishes do not get damaged, but use what you would like to use. (Your group may have purchased paper items, check with coordinator.)

Things Hostess Needs: *The Harvey Girls* movie, place settings for table including napkins, silverware, dishes and glasses, centerpiece (use anything you have), candlesticks, salt & pepper, menu.

Demonstration of Skill: Have a formal place setting laid out, and explain it. This, of course, is for very formal company, or feasts not often practiced anymore. It is still a skill that each lady should know if she is able to present hospitality under all circumstances, especially in helping families on formal occasions such as holidays. Ask the girls to practice setting the table but always leave your one setting as a reference.

*   **Teach the first rule to remember easily:** The first item used for the meal will be on the outside. So one must know what will be served to know what silverware, dishes and glasses are needed and where to place them. Prepare a menu including salad, soup and a first course followed by dinner and dessert. Also, include bread and butter as part of the meal. Wine and champagne will be served as well as coffee/tea. Tell them to look at the menu to see what will be necessary to set the table and explain it.

* **The Basics** - The forks always go to the left of the plate in order of how they will be used. The knife and spoons will be placed to the right of the plate, with blade facing in towards the plate, followed by any spoons that will be used for the meal. The teaspoon is placed next to the knife, and the soup spoon, next to that. Note the drawing on page 47 for guidance on the setting. The napkin is best placed to the left of the fork. (When it is placed under the fork, it is awkward for the user to get to, without upsetting all the forks. Sometimes it is placed on the plate but this also is awkward.) The dessert spoon and fork are placed above the plate between the butter plate and glasses.

* **Glasses** - the water glass goes above the knife followed in descending order: water, champagne, wine, and although coffee is next, this is placed directly to the right of the spoons. Often coffee is not served until after the meal and the cups are placed at that time.

* **Plates** - For formal dinners, charger plates are placed in the center of the place setting upon which all other plates will be placed. Nowadays, in home settings, many do not own these, so teach it either way. *A very important rule for plates: all dishes are always to be served on a plate. This goes for soup bowls, dessert bowls and parfait glasses. Never bring in soup without a plate under it. This goes for informal settings as well. Many people don't know this. Next rule: the bread and butter plate is to be placed to the left of the forks, but, unless you are the Queen of England and have an eighty-foot table, this may not be practical. In this case, place it in the center above, just to the left of the water glass and place the butter knife across it. (Teach them where it should go, but then show them where most people put it because of lack of space.)

* **Once the table is set, there are things that should be in place immediately before guests are seated.** A pat of butter should be placed on each butter plate. Water is to fill the water glasses being careful not to spill on the tablecloth. Salt and pepper should be placed at either end of the table in the center. Some sort of low centerpiece is to be placed in the center so as not to obstruct conversation across the table.

Practice of Skill: Leave one place setting as a reference and ask each girl to set additional place settings until all settings are done. If there are more girls than settings, remove some, and rotate girls from watchers to setters, until all girls have practiced.

Then show what goes in the middle and how it is arranged. Candles, salt & pepper, butter, if bread will be served, are all placed in the center. Butter can either be placed on a central plate already sliced, or pieces of butter can be placed ahead of time for guests on their individual butter plates.

Do not forget a centerpiece which often brings the most beauty to the table, but do not place anything that would obstruct the view of the person across the table. Many hostesses get a magnificent centerpiece with beautiful gladiolas, but it is not very inviting, because you can't talk with the person across the table since the flowers are blocking them. Once this is done, the girls can move onto service. Have some girls sit as if at the meal, while you show everyone how to bring in a plate and set it down, and then, how to remove it when done. Remind the girls that you know when someone is done by how they lay their silverware across the plate. The knife and fork should be placed together across the top right of the plate to signal "done."

SERVICE & REMOVAL: Make certain the girls learn the rule: On to the left, off to the right. This is the main rule of serving and clearing a table at a meal. When the meal is served, you place the meal onto the left of the person. When the meal is over, a server quietly takes the plate off to the right. A server should never stack plates. Simply take one plate off to the right, transfer to the left hand, go to the next person and remove another plate. Bring these to the kitchen before taking anything else from the table. Always serve and remove from ladies first.

Once all has been removed from the table, attend to the center. Remove anything having to do with dinner such as salt and pepper and butter (not the centerpiece or candles). Take off the butter and the rolls and any food remaining which has to do with the main meal. All that should remain after clearing are the lit candles, the centerpiece, napkins, glasses and those pieces of silverware needed to finish the meal. Everything else goes, quietly and discreetly. A server should never make clearing the table, the event. The conversation should be the event. If you are not certain if someone is finished, wait until they're done talking and quietly ask, "Excuse me, are you finished?"

Remember we are serving others to help foster hospitality, making others welcome. In many cases, it may be to help out our parents with guests. Try to focus on the job and not on the conversation, as it is not necessarily our business.

Next, bring in the dessert! That's what we've all been waiting for, right? Place the plate down to the left of each guest. Have someone go around with coffee cups with saucers and place to the right of the guests. Another girl can quietly place a sugar and creamer at each end of the table. Finally, a girl can quietly go around with a coffee server asking each guest if they would care for some. It's done. The final clearing can occur once the guests have left the table.

Showing the final step: show a very informal setting with just a fork, knife, glass and napkin that would be used for a weeknight dinner. Remind the girls that the basic rules remain the same, no matter how many pieces or courses are served.

Fun Games: (If time allows)

1. Using paper plates and cups, etc. so nothing good gets broken, have a separate table set up or team off for each side of the table and have the girls race to see who can set the table the quickest. Make teams for ease of time. Take points off for incorrect placement.

2. Another fun relay using plastic plates would be to line the girls up in two teams each with a plastic plate. Set a distance ahead that they need to walk to with the plate on there head, and return from, without the plate falling off. The plate gets handed to the next girl, etc. The first team to complete the relay wins. To make it more challenging, add in, carrying a spoon with something on it, while having the plate on their head. We have also added a plastic cup on top the plate while carrying the spoon with something in it. It can be done and is so much fun for the girls. Don't forget to take pictures!

Conclusion: Once everyone has had a turn at serving and removing, ask the girls if they have any questions. Talk about occasions for using this skill, and focus the girls on the simpler idea, that this can be used at home every night. We do not have to wait for a special occasion nor do we have to set a formal place setting with good china. Manners and service can always be used to help another at our own home or at another's. Pray a closing prayer that we can use our new skill to help others.

Take Home:

* Practice setting the table at home for a week and clearing the spots for everyone when done.

* Ask your mother if you can use her good china to set a nice table for two, for your mom and dad, and volunteer to serve a "date night" for them. Don't forget the candles and a centerpiece. What a treat that would be for them! You could do the dishes when you aren't serving, so they could enjoy a relaxing evening. Depending on the time of year, maybe you can gather some wildflowers for your centerpiece.

* Get some friends together to play restaurant. Make some menus using some cookbooks and set the tables. Some can be the customers, and some be the servers. Plan ahead and ask your mom if you can serve some real food.

* Plan a night to have popcorn and watch *The Harvey Girls* with Judy Garland.

* If a major holiday or formal party is taking place, ask your mom if you can help set the table and serve. Remember to be extra careful when handling your mom's good china and crystal and never stack the dishes.

FIELD TRIPS:

1. Go to tea at a formal tea house and notice how the table is set, and how the food is served.

2. Go to a department store, in the china department, and arrange for someone to show you how to properly set a place setting. Browse through the china, crystal and fine silver. Have everyone pick out their favorite pattern and write it down. If the store has sample pictures of the patterns, have the girls take one and put it in their binders. They can see if their taste stayed the same when it is time to buy their china when they get married.

3. Offer to serve or help with a charity dinner. The pro-life movement usually has many occasions when servers are needed.

Recommended Reading: A good etiquette book; *The Harvey House Cookbook*; there are even now a set of Harvey Girl paper dolls.

Movies: *The Harvey Girls* with Judy Garland (Excellent and funny about the historical

Fred Harvey houses that civilized the West with hospitality, white tablecloths and meticulous dining rooms, and well-mannered girls.)

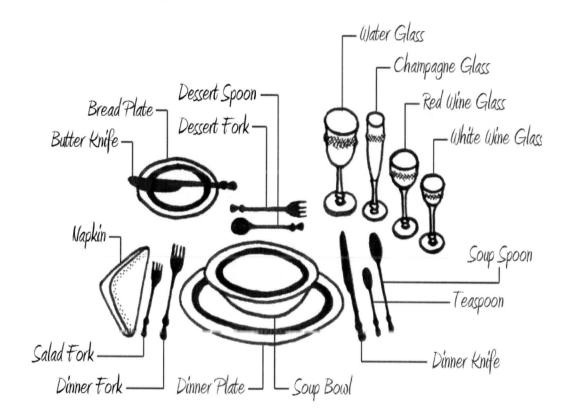

Hospitality: Table Manners, Conversation and How to Treat Others

"Do unto others as you would have them do unto you." Luke 6:31

Holy Inspiration:

Martha and Mary are a good example for us today to teach us how to treat others. Jesus is a guest in their home and Martha decides to treat Him to a wonderful dinner. She runs to prepare something she thinks he will like while Mary sits to visit with Him. Martha is trying to be a hospitable hostess in preparing the food but is upset with her sister for not helping. Martha is no longer giving of herself joyfully. Our Lord tells Martha that Mary has chosen the better part. This is hard for us to understand since we think work is better than sitting. Here Our Lord reminds us that our time with Him is so limited, we do not want to throw it away doing unnecessary work. This is a good reminder for us at Mass to sit with Our Lord and talk with Him. We don't want to be distracted by those around us or what friends we see at Mass or what everyone is wearing. Just sit and enjoy our Lord's company.

Our manners, as a hostess in our home, also require us to sit with our guest and visit, whether at a table or not, and to prepare something simple so as to enjoy them. Let us always pray before our visits that we may enjoy our friends and are able to converse and listen in a way that is kind and helpful. Did you know when we visit with another, if we do it in a charitable way, this is a part of the virtue of hospitality? This is the part Our Lord was explaining to us that Mary portrayed. Let us pray that we may learn this skill of good conversation and manners of how to behave when at a table.

Our Lady's Patronage: Our Lady, under the title Seat of Wisdom, will help us practice this aspect of our virtue of hospitality. Let us turn to her especially when we are engaged in conversation with others. Let her lead us to always speak charitably, avoid gossip, help others feel at ease in our company. In this way, like Our Lady, we lead others to Christ through our Christian word and example.

Charm: Circle of Friends

Literature Example: In the American Girl's book, *Felicity*, by Valerie Tripp, Felicity is taught how to become a "gentle woman" or a lady, as we may call her. One of the skills needed to become an accomplished lady is to learn proper table manners. In colonial times, girls were enrolled in a class very much like this one, to learn from a respected, and accomplished "gentle woman." Here is a passage from the chapter entitled "Loose Tooth Tea."

"Hand each guest her cup, saucer and spoon," Miss Manderly said, as she did so.

"And when the tea is ready, pour it very carefully." Felicity held her teacup and saucer steady as Miss Manderly filled it. "Offer your guest milk or sugar to put in her tea," said Miss Manderly.

"Then offer her a cake or a biscuit."

"Oh, these are queen cakes!' said Annabelle as she took a small cake filled with currants from the plate. 'I have heard they are a favorite of the queen of England."

Miss Manderly held the plate of biscuits and queen cakes out to Felicity. Felicity took the smallest biscuit she saw. Miss Manderly smiled. "A wise choice. Hard biscuits don't shed crumbs the way cakes do," she said, "And remember, you are not drinking tea because you are thirsty or eating because you are hungry. The tea is offered to you as a sign of your hostess' hospitality. If you refuse tea, you are refusing her generosity."

"Oh, I would never refuse!" Felicity said. "You make the tea ceremony look so very pretty."

"Thank you, my dear," smiled Miss Manderly. "But you may not wish to drink tea all afternoon! There is of course a polite way to show that you have had enough tea. Merely turn your cup upside down on your saucer and place your spoon across it. That is a signal to your hostess that you do not wish to take more tea. And the correct phrase to say is, 'Thank you. I shall take no tea.' "

Discussion: What important lessons does Felicity learn in this passage? Let the girls discuss it and see what their replies may be. Pay particular attention to how they converse and listen to each other, waiting to talk and, most importantly, not interrupting another. At this point, also draw attention to how one should sit as a lady if you notice any of the girls not sitting the way a lady should sit. Don't single out any particular girl and embarrass her, just ask all to watch you as you properly show them how to sit.

Conclusion from Passage: If they did not arrive at this, tell them Felicity learned that there is a certain way to act and behave when at a table. There is a proper way to do things, just as with our Faith, and rules that can guide us, so we might enjoy ourselves and become little gentle women.

The Lesson

Notes to the Hostess: Have a table set ahead of time, maybe even a card table, to practice table manners. Make some place settings formal and some informal. It is not necessary to bring out your good china but be sure to include all the pieces indicated in the diagram on page 47. Attached is the lesson for setting a table to use as a reference. By all means, use paper utensils and plates to demonstrate this skill. Your group may actually already provide these. It would be a shame to have your personal china settings damaged as a result of teaching.

Put a few things in the center that the girls could pass, like a basket of bread or rolls, something you can scoop with a spoon like cereal, and a plate with pieces of bread (meat) to practice with a large fork. You decide what food to use. The point is to practice serving and passing, not eating, although I'm sure we'd all like to practice that more.

Things Hostess Needs: Table set up as above, cards with different situations written out for role play practice. Ideas can include: eating at a formal dinner like Thanksgiving, eat at a casual dinner, introductions of people when guests don't all know each other, casual conversation when girls get together - make up things to talk about like favorite foods, fun games, etc. Items needed for place settings and food, a timer for role plays and cards with situation to be acted out.

Demonstration:
This lesson is broken into two parts: Table Manners and Conversation. Although they are intertwined, set aside time to practice just taking, passing and eating with the right utensils. Then set role play up for conversation, both at the table and away from it.

WATCH YOUR TIME, it will go quickly and you want to fit everything in.

I. Table Manners: Sit yourself at the table with the girls gathered around you. You will need another girl or mom at the table to pass to and play off of, but you are the lead for the demonstration.

1. All sit at once and put your napkin on your lap. Begin by explaining the order of your glasses and silverware so each girl knows what each piece is used for and when. Tell them you never begin to eat or serve yourself until everyone is seated, especially the hostess, unless she tells you to. When food is served family style and placed on the table, offer it to the person next to you before yourself.

2. Then, "hostess" begins by asking the person across from her to pass the rolls. She takes a roll and places it on her butter plate. Then she passes it to the right. Show the girls that all items are to be passed to the right. You wait until an item is passed to you. If it is in the course of the meal and everything has been passed and placed in the center, then you may ask quietly for an item. Do not reach for it or interrupt anyone to get it. ABOVE ALL, be patient! Many people unfortunately forget this and think of only what they want, not that someone is talking and they are rudely interrupting.

3. **Salad:** Have a salad plate nearby that should be placed in front of you. Show them which fork to use and then show them how to place the fork across the top when done. Wow, two utensils down, whew!

4. **Soup:** Next, have a small plate with a soup bowl nearby: select the cereal and announce it is the soup. Show them how to properly eat with a soup spoon and when it is done, place spoon on the side of smaller plate under soup bowl. Remind the girls: do not pick up a bowl and drink from it. Explain that when the soup is cleared before the main meal, the little plate is removed with the bowl, not just the bowl.

5. **Main entrée:** Ask to have the "meat" passed to you. Take a piece with the fork and gently place it on your plate. Explain that we only take one piece, and we do not stab it. We want to make sure there is enough for everybody. We gently poke it and if it doesn't release easily on our plate we may use one of our utensils to slide it off. Never use your hands during the meal, always use another utensil especially to push smaller pieces onto your fork. (You could use some cereal to demonstrate this). Next, slice meat, place knife down at top of meat, switch hands and eat. We are Americans so we are taught to eat American as is the custom. European style of eating can be done well by people who have been taught, but others who try it and are not use to it, end up looking like the food is being shoved into their mouth. Pass the meat or place it down. Always cut meat and other food into small pieces. Never shove a huge piece into your mouth. You shouldn't talk with food in your mouth, but a good rule of thumb is, that the piece of food in your mouth should be small enough that you could talk.

6. **The dinner is over.** Place fork and knife across top of plate to indicate you are done. These are the rules Felicity was being taught. Your server will then know it is ok to remove your plate. Show them that you are not done when the fork is placed across the left side and knife on right side instead of both placed together across far side of plate.

7. **One fork should be left for dessert.** Tell them they get the idea and begin to practice with them.

50

8. **Table Conversation:** Join in the table conversation. Food is a way of bringing people together especially on formal occasions not just to attain sustenance but to visit and deepen our friendships, interest and knowledge.

II. Conversation- Now it is time to teach about conversation which will be used at the table or anywhere else.

Have two girls stand with you as you demonstrate how to introduce others and make everyone feel included. Pretend neither girl knows each other but you know they both like horses. "Hello, Mary, this is Jenny. Jenny, this is Mary. Did you know you both enjoyed horses?" This is a way to make people who don't know each other feel comfortable by showing them something they have in common. Once they feel at ease talking, they'll learn other things they have in common or enjoy. We always want to make others feel included in our conversation, not left out. This is a vital point to make about the virtue of hospitality and making others feel welcome. This is what it is all about. As people grow older, we want to practice thinking about others in our conversation because as our lives get busier, we forget to include others and girls' feelings can be hurt very easily not just by what we say, but sometimes by what we don't say. If we feel comfortable because we know everyone, sometimes we don't make an effort to notice the person who is left out. **Our Lord calls us through the virtue of hospitality to seek out the lonely and to include them just as He did.** *(Please make an extra effort to bring this point home with the girls. Too often, girls leave others out or make them feel as if they are not good enough, cool enough or smart enough. Explain that we never should feel better than someone else in any way.)*

Teach how to start a conversation - Sometimes we want to visit with each other but don't know how:

1. **Plan ahead whether you're the host or the guest.** Always say a prayer before you join others that you will enjoy the company you are with and that nice things are spoken about. "Holy Spirit, guide us in our conversation." Simple and to the point. Then, think of four or five subjects you could discuss with the person or people you will be visiting with. "What do you want to talk about," although polite, often ends up in a game of saying it back and forth until no one cares to talk at all. It is often helpful to start conversation and makes others at ease. Just because you start the conversation does not mean you are putting yourself first. Once the conversation has taken off then.....

2. **Never Interrupt-** No one likes a word hog. It is certainly not polite and makes others feel like you don't think that what they have to say is important. A good rule of thumb is if you go home not having learned much, you probably talked too much. Just try harder next time.

3. **Talk about something that would interest the other (or if it is a big group), that all can participate in:** Things to talk about: Books, Games, People (good things), Vacations, Hikes, Sports, Food, Movies, Clothes, Church, Activities in which you may be involved.

4. **Being a Good Listener** - Conversation means con (together) + vertere (to turn) = to turn a line together. Listening is just as important as talking. Remember conversation is turning the line together. This is especially important when a friend needs you to listen when she is down or needs advice, to cheer them up when they need that. Sometimes conversation is our tool to further our friendship with others through interesting and fun ideas. This is a valuable and fun way to serve others through our friendship.

5. ***Including Others** - We spoke about this above but let us add this to the rules for good conversation. If you can't think of something to say then just ask the person to come sit next to you. A gesture can often make someone feel just as included. Or "Mary, what do you think about this? You always have nice things to say." Help draw out shy people. Don't put them on the spot but gently bring them into the conversation or maybe change the subject if everyone can't participate. "Why don't we talk about _____, I don't think everyone is familiar with what is being discussed now." Kindness is the key to including others but don't do it at the expense of being rude to the ones talking. Just wait until it is your turn to talk.

6. **Games:** If a large group is getting together, games are always a fun way to break the ice and get everyone having fun whether or not they know each other. So always learn a good indoor or outdoor game you can play in any circumstance. You can suggest it as either host or guest if you see the need.

Practice: Much of the lesson will be learned through practicing. Take some notes so when the role play is done, you may comment if things should have gone differently.

Do five minute Role Play of the different situations below: Ask two, three or more girls to be at the front and give them the situation and time five minutes on your timer to let them do the role play. Have the others watch and critique afterwards for a minute on what was good or not so good about how they treated each other. Switch girls and do another.

1. **Five Girls Needed** - Girls are arriving for a birthday party with gifts in hand. Three of the girls know each other but two are acquaintances from soccer and the other from ballet.

2. **Four Girls** meet up at a friend's house and one girl doesn't think that the two

girls are being very nice to the fourth girl.

3.   **Four Girls** are placed at the table. Tell them lunch is just being served. Begin.

4.   **Three Girls** are working on an art project for school together. Two girls are very good artists but the third girl makes a mess of the project. She was trying to do her best but art is just not her talent.

5.   **Two Girls** meet for the first time at a class. They are sitting waiting for the activity to begin.

6.   **Four Girls** are playing outside having a fun time playing tag. There is a new girl next door their age who is sitting doing chalk on her driveway right next to where the girls are playing.

Add more role plays of your own if needed.

Additional Activities:

Guess Who Game: Take index cards and write famous people familiar to the group on them. Then pin them to the back of the girls and they walk around asking questions about themselves. The first girl to guess the name on their back, wins. Suggestions: Saints, Literature characters like Felicity, Laura Ingalls, Mrs. Oleson, historical figures like Florence Nightingale or Betsy Ross. This is really a fun game.

Conclusion: Ask everyone how they learned about manners and how to treat one another. Close with a prayer and invite the girls to snack.

TAKE HOME:

* Practice your table manners with your family or friends. Invite some friends over for a casual get together and try out your new hostess skills. Serve tea and cookies.

* Take some time to play a game with a sibling you don't often do something for or ask if they want to hang out in your room for awhile.

* Think about your manners at table or on the phone and work on improving one thing about them.

* Make up conversation cards for the dinner table that everyone can pick up and answer for a fun dinner. "Table Talk" is a card game available that does this. It makes dinner time include everyone in the conversation. Remember to listen to your younger siblings. Sometimes they get left out of the conversation.

* Go out of your way to talk with someone who doesn't get many visitors or calls, maybe an elderly person you know, a friend who is shy or someone else you can think of. This is a great way to practice serving others and getting closer to Our Lord and Lady. Think of how good you can make someone else feel.

FIELD TRIPS:
* Look into a place that serves high tea and see if they moms/daughters of your group would like to meet. Practice table manners and conversation at the table.

* Have a daddy/daughter dance in someone's home and practice the skills of conversation. Maybe even see if you can plan some dance lessons like Felicity had.

Recommended Reading: *Felicity* and *Samantha* books by Valerie Tripp, Jane Austen novels (for older girls)

Movies: *Felicity: An American Girl Adventure, Sense and Sensibility* (older girls)

Hospitality: The Skill of Preparing a Room for a Guest

"They must enjoy having guests in their home and must love all that is good." Titus 1:8

Holy Inspiration: *The Nativity*- When St. Joseph and Our Lady arrived at the stable after a very long journey, they were tired, hungry and cold. They had just been turned out from every inn and home in which they sought shelter. Very little hospitality was shown to them as they carried and awaited the arrival of our Messiah, our Savior. Mary and Joseph did not dwell on the bad things that others had done to them. They turned to Our Lord as their focus as we should always do. They needed to make a warm place for Jesus to be born. Gratefully, they accepted one man's kindness and use of his stable. St. Joseph had Mary sit and rest. He piled up some hay and there Mary slept while Joseph set out to clean the stable.

Remember, a stable is a very messy and awful smelling place. This is where the animals are kept and fed. Joseph himself, being a carpenter, probably didn't own animals or a stable, but he still knew exactly what to do. He cleaned out every corner from the mess the animals had made. He took a trough, a feeding box for the animals, and cleaned it out and scrubbed it, until it was as clean as it could be. Next, he cleared out the center of the stable and moved any animals that needed to vacate this space. He needed plenty of room for Mary and the baby, and enough room for visitors that would come to see their King. He did not have much, but he still made a warm room for Mary, and baby Jesus, to be hospitable to others.

Lastly, he placed the clean trough, the manger, and filled it with fresh straw and laid some of the blankets Mary and St. Anne had no doubt sewn for the new baby. When Mary awoke, it was time for Our Lord to come. She was much comforted to have a clean room in which to welcome Him.

Our Lady's Patronage: We put this skill under the patronage of the Our Lady of the Holy Family. Her example of quiet, dedicated service to her family is an example for all women. She was obedient to St. Joseph, a mother and teacher to Christ, and a servant to both. When we think of the times she must have cooked a meal, made a bed, cleaned a room for her family, we can see how these acts can truly be given to God through her hands. Let us practice this skill as if the Christ Child himself is looking for a room at our house.

Charm: Cabin

Literature Example: From *The Singing Tree* by Kate Seredy, the sequel book to *The Good Master.* Everyone shows hospitality to a new married couple on their wedding day. The wedding was over and…

The climax of all Hungarian weddings, the "Lead Me Home," had begun. Men loaded all the bride's belongings into wagons. First came the freshly painted, gay new furniture. Then came homespun linens, sheets, pillowcases, curtains, tablecloths - dozens of everything, the product of twenty years of spinning, weaving, sewing. Dishes, cooking utensils, wooden implements came next, filling another wagon to the brim. The next one was loaded with food, bags and barrels of it. After all Mari's belongings had been packed into wagons, the guests piled into their own vehicles and the long procession began. The gypsies went ahead, playing favorite old songs and marches all the way. Each following wagon was lighted by six torches, except the last one, in which Mari and Peter were riding. The young couple were being led home; they didn't need a light - there was half a mile of blazing light and heart-warming music to follow.

Peter's farm was quite a distance from the village, and by the time he and Mari arrived the house was ready for them. Furniture had been placed, the bed made, the table set for two; the guests had even fed the chickens, pigs, and the cow. When Mari and Peter alighted, the first "caller" took them by the hand and led them over the threshold. They stood there, inside their home, waiting for the parting words of the caller; words without which no wedding was complete. Again the guests stood in half-circle and the caller began to speak.

"Peter and Mari Hodi, may the Lord bless you and your home. May the Lord give you good health and happiness, long life, peace and prosperity, and may He send you children, grandchildren, and great-grandchildren, as many as there are stars in the sky."

He reached for the doorknob, and as he closed the door he said: "May this door keep all worry, all sadness and strife out of your house forever and after. Good night."

Discussion: How was the virtue of hospitality practiced in this passage about this newly married Hungarian couple? Do you like this tradition? What makes it so beautiful? (Let the girls discuss this.)

Possible answers: Simplicity is one reason why the beauty stands out. The generosity of all the townspeople, giving their "20 years of spinning, weaving, sewing" to this new couple, who probably had nothing, should inspire us all. Notice the care and love with which they prepared this new home for this couple. They made sure they had everything they needed, and all the details were attended to so that each room was properly equipped to start their new home. We should treat our guests in a similar way, making sure they are comfortable and all their needs are met. Yet, hospitality calls for us to go beyond basic needs and asks of us to serve in a more detailed manner. We need to attend to the "little extras" that make a person feel at home and comfortable in our home.

The Lesson

Note to Hostess: This lesson has many steps and is a primary lesson so plan ahead and pace yourself. Keep the girls focused so you don't run out of time. Hospitality should always be fun, so don't be a slave driver with the beds, just try to have them make a neat, tight and tidy bed.

Things Hostess Needs: Bedroom, clean sheets, blankets and comforter, set of towels (more for practicing), baskets with sample bottles, note paper or index cards, pencils, bag of mints to distribute to girls for family members' pillows (noted in Take Home), any items chosen from "personal touches" or "fun extras" part from below.

Demonstration: The hostess or teaching mom will take the girls through the steps of cleaning and preparing the guest room. Pay particular attention to the bed making since this skill is necessary for the girls to learn and practice on their own beds. Take care to show the squaring of the corners and placing the sheets on the correct way. Teach the points below in order and your room will be perfectly prepared.

* **Remind them of the Skills they learned to clean a room:** dusting, vacuuming- Cleaning the room would be first. Inform them because of time today we will pretend we cleaned it and move on.

* **How to Make a Bed (Best done on a twin bed to learn).**

1. First make certain you always have clean sheets including clean pillow cases

2. Begin with a stripped bed and demonstrate how to put on fitted sheets. Remember to tell the girls the names of the sheets, fitted and top, as you show them. Next place the top sheet face down, so that when the blanket is placed on top and tucked in, the top of the sheet can be folded back to show the right side. After the top sheet and blanket are layered, teach the girls how to do a square corner on both sides of the bottom. Tuck the sheet and blanket in all along the bottom, and then square the corners. This is similar to wrapping a package when you fold and wrap the ends, and tuck them under.

3. Next show them how to find the correct spot on a comforter or bedside for top and bottom. The bottom and sides always have some sort of edging but not on the top. Place top layer on and smooth out with hard motions with side of hands.

4. Once the bed is basically made, place all the pillows back on, in order of sleeping, topped with decorative. Place an extra folded blanket at bottom of bed or folded and placed over side chair or table if guest gets cold.

* **How to Straighten a Room for guests -** Make certain that no family extras are around: no toys, games, etc. are left out from kids playing in the room. Tell them to empty at least the top drawer or drawers of a dresser to make room for the guests clothing and remove the items in the drawer from the room. Check the closet so it is not full, and that there are plenty of available hangers for the guest to use. Check the floor and shelf to remove any clutter or items that may "fall out" when opened.

* **HOSTESS**: Prepare your closet so that it has tons of stuff so you can demonstrate what to remove and the girls can practice de-cluttering. Everyone uses their guest room closet to store all their extras or change of season clothes.

* **Clear tops of low dresser, side table or desk for guest to place luggage on to open.**

* **Leave clean towels for guests stacked neatly or in a nice basket.** Baskets are nice if it is a small room and table space is limited, it can be placed on the floor. Otherwise, towels can be folded neatly and placed on desk/dresser top or on foot of the bed. Teach girls how to fold a towel. Lay flat, fold one side to middle, then other side, then fold in threes, using side of hand to take out wrinkles with each fold. Each set of towels per guest should include a bath towel, a hand towel and a washcloth. Show them these and their names.

* **Items to have in room:** Alarm clock, nightlight if they need to get up in the middle of the night, water glass and pitcher, or small unopened water bottles, small dish to hold coins, earrings, etc., and a folded bag for dirty laundry.

* **Personal Touches-** Have a basket with fun items or things the guest may have forgotten: small toothpaste, toothbrush, lotion, shampoo, soap, maybe even a note card with envelope and stamp tied with a ribbon and pen for a note to someone at home or postcard of your town. You could even put a disposable camera in it. These baskets can be prepared much ahead and kept in storage for when guests come. Planning ahead is a great tip for always having things ready to practice hospitality. Sometimes we don't always know ahead when a guest will stay. It will also make it easier to invite someone to stay when you know your room is already prepared.

* **Fun extras:** Have fresh flowers in the room, put a mint on the pillow (have a basket of mints for the girls), a note to say hello and welcome, or a special quote, prayer or poem to make the guest feel special. (These are so easily done on the computer and printed on cardstock.) Also, place some seasonal magazines or one's the guest would enjoy. You don't have to run out and buy the latest one. Keep a supply of garden, cooking, travel, history or science magazines. They don't have to be new to be interesting. Also, place a few books from your

home library that you think your guest would enjoy.

Practice: Do as much as you can. It may not all get done. Don't worry.

* **BEDS:** Have each of the girls practice making a bed. *If it is a large group of girls, have them make the bed in pairs, one girl on each side. Strip it down after each girl. Alternate between this and folding towels making sure that each layer of the bed and towels is tight and smooth. No one wants it to look used or slept in. This would be an appropriate time to fold sheets or blankets as well.

* **FOLDING SHEETS and BLANKETS:** Teach girls how to fold sheets or blankets using two girls. Each girl stands and holds corners of sheets(or blankets) and folds in half. Grab corners and fold in half again. Then, one girl walks to the other. The one girl takes all four corners together, lays the sheet or blanket on the bed for the last one or two folds. Remember to tuck the folds hard when making the fold. You should now have a beautifully folded blanket or sheet. Practice folding towels in threes as well at this point. Directions are included in demonstration part above.

* **A TIDY DRAWER:** If needed, teach the girls how to keep a neat drawer. Bring one out already prepared. Show them tricks of how to roll socks together or pin them so the drawer stays organized. The basic rule is to put like with likes. Put shirts in one drawer, pants in another, etc. Folding for clothes is similar to folding towels. You can demonstrate a shirt. Fold with one half to center, then the other half and fold over in two or three. I also like the "army roll." Fold shirt, pants or shorts in half, then from the top, tightly roll down tucking and smoothing as you go. The advantage to this method for drawers is that you can fit more in one row and be able to see all your shirts at once. (It's also great for packing.)

* **Further: CLOSET ORGANIZATION:** Teach girls to group their clothes by color, this way it makes it easy to grab the color you need for an outfit. It also presents a lovely closet.

Concluding Discussion: This is just to remind the girls that this new skill is part of the virtue of hospitality. Ask them, how can they use this new skill to serve others? If there is no time for discussion, just leave it for something for them to think about as you read to them their assignments for practicing this skill at home from the Take Home sheet. Pass out the mints to the girls to take home for their siblings and parents pillows at night. End with a prayer.

Take Home:

* Practice making your bed at home and volunteer to make another family member's bed. Maybe your mom can show you how to wash and dry the sheets so each day you can clean and change a different bed in your house. By the end of the week, your own parents and siblings will feel like guests at a hotel.

* Please take a mint for each member of your family and leave it on their pillow with a nice note one evening. It will be a wonderful way for you to extend this virtue of hospitality to someone in your own family and at the end of a long day, they will be very thankful.

* Another way to practice this month's skill is to help a younger sibling clean his/her room. Don't just do it all for them but teach them the skill of how to put things away so they can be proud of their own work. Bring in a bin for all the extras that don't belong in their room.

* Straighten your own drawers and closets. Get rid of toys or clothes you don't use or fit.

* Practice folding blankets, towels and sheets for storage. Ask your mom or sibling to hold the other end, it makes it a lot easier. Remember: Each girl stands and holds corners of sheets (or blankets) and folds in half. Grab corners and fold in half again. Then, one girl walks to the other. The one girl takes all four corners together, lays the sheet or blanket on the bed for the last one or two folds. Remember to tuck the folds hard when making the fold. You should now have a beautifully folded blanket or sheet ready for the linen closet.

Field Trip Ideas:

Virtue: Service to Others: Help another mom who may have just had a baby or who is struggling with a sick member of their family. See if you can arrange for an afternoon to go to their home and help clean and straighten their rooms. What a refreshing thing that would be for them, to go to their rooms with well-made beds to climb into. If the mom in need is someone who likes to clean herself, then volunteer to play with the children or do a craft or game with them for a couple hours to free her time to do so.

HOTEL OUTING: Mom: Call a local hotel like Residence Inn by Marriot and see if they could arrange for a "home-economics" class to come and see how a professional cleans and prepares a room for a guest. Then maybe everyone could stop for hot chocolate or ice cream in the hotel restaurant.

Recommended Reading: *The Good Master* and *The Singing Tree* by Kate

Seredy. In *The Good Master*, a Budapest family makes room in their home and hearts, for a very spoiled niece, and transform her through love, hard work, the great outdoors and the simple things reaped from being part of a family. *The Singing Tree* is the sequel from which this lesson was taken. Everyone will enjoy both stories. You will be left wanting more.

Hospitality: The Skill of Correspondence

Holy Inspiration: *The Epistles*, in the New Testament, are a great inspiration for us. They show us the importance of good correspondence. Some of the apostles and disciples of Our Lord used the gift of writing to spread the gospel and the life of Christ to people they could not be with on a daily basis. These letters or epistles as they are called, continue to teach us today many valuable lessons, and keep us focused on the truths that Our Lord came to tell us. They make us see a part of God's kingdom and our call to be in it, as we read our favorites, or listen to the ones laid out at Mass as part of our liturgical year. The Popes through the ages have written letters to us, the members of the Church, to express many of the beautiful treasures that our families and Faith hold for us. Letters have always been a great teaching tool for the Church.

Our Lady's Patronage: As apostles by Baptism, we have to learn to communicate the Good News effectively. Our Lady of the Apostles will be our patron while we practice this skill. Her example and inpiration have been penned by the apostles and those first disciples of Christ, even though any writings directly penned by her are unknown. Today, as in the past, she inspires great saints to spread her Son's words. Let us ask her intercession as we write our family and friends and practice the skill of correspondence.

Charm: Pencil

Literature Example of Letter Writing: G.K. Chesterton depicts a mailbox as "a sanctuary of human words-the place to which friends…commit their messages, confident that when they have done that they are secret, except to future biographers- not to be touched by hands, not even by time… A letter is one of the few things left entirely romantic, for to be entirely romantic, a thing must be irrevocable."

Louisa May Alcott, master of writing herself, speaks of letters as a connection to her loved ones bringing much awaited good news and sentiments in her book *Little Women.*

News from their father comforted them very much….Mr. Brooke sent a bulletin every day, and as the head of the family, Meg insisted on reading the dispatches, which grew more and more cheering as the week passed. At first, everyone was eager to write, and plump envelopes were carefully poked into the letter box by one or other of the sisters, who felt rather important with their Washington correspondence. As one of these packets contained characteristic notes from the party, we will rob an imaginary mail, and read them:

"My dearest Mother:
It is impossible to tell you how happy your last letter made

us, for the news was so good we couldn't help laughing and crying over it. How very kind Mr. Brooke is, and how fortunate that Mr. Laurence's business detains him near you so long, since he is so useful to you and father. The girls are as good as gold. Jo helps me with the sewing, and insists on doing all sorts of hard jobs. I should be afraid she might overdo, if I didn't know that her 'moral fit' wouldn't last long. Beth is as regular about her tasks as a clock, and never forgets what you told her. She grieves about father, and is sober except when she is at her little piano. Amy minds me nicely, and I take great care of her. She does her own hair and I am teaching her to make buttonholes and mend stockings. She tries very hard, and I know you will be pleased with her improvement when you come. Mr. Laurence watches over us like a motherly old hen, as Jo says; and Laurie is very kind and neighborly. He and Jo keep us merry, for we get pretty blue sometimes, and feel like orphans with you so far away. Hannah is a perfect saint; she does not scold at all, and always calls me 'Miss Margaret,' which is quite proper, you know, and treats me with respect. We are all well and busy; but we long, day and night, to have you back. Give my dearest love to father, and believe me,

Ever your own,
Meg"

This note, prettily written on scented paper, was a great contrast to the next, which scribbled on a big sheet of thin foreign paper, ornamented with blots and all manner of flourishes and curly-tailed letters:

'My precious Marmee:

Three cheers for dear father! Brooke was a trump to telegraph right off, and let us know the minute he was better. I rushed up garret when the letter came, and tried to thank God for being so good to us; but I could only cry, and say, 'I'm glad! I'm glad!' Didn't that do as well as a regular prayer? For I felt a great many in my heart. We have such funny times; and now I can enjoy them, for everyone is so desperately good, it's like living in a nest of turtledoves. You'd laugh to see Meg every day, and I'm in love with her sometimes. The children are regular archangels, and I - well, I'm Jo, and never shall be anything else.
Oh, I must tell you that I came near having a quarrel with Laurie. I freed my mind about a silly little thing, and he was offended. I was right, but didn't speak as I ought, begged pardon. I declared I wouldn't, and got mad. It lasted all day; I felt bad, and wanted you very much. Laurie and I are both so proud, it's hard to beg pardon; but I thought he'd come to it, for I was in the right. He didn't come; and just at night I remembered what you said when Amy fell into the river. I read my little book, felt better, resolved not to let the sun set on my anger, and ran over to tell Laurie I was sorry. I met him at the gate, coming for the same thing. We both laughed, begged each other's pardon, and felt all good and comfortable

again.

I made a 'poem' yesterday, when I was helping Hannah wash; and, as father likes silly little things, I put it in to amuse him. Give him the lovingest hug that ever was, and kiss yourself a dozen times,

for your,
Topsy-Turvy Jo.'

Discussion: Ask the girls how they enjoyed the letters and how they differed. Didn't they feel like they got to know these two sisters just from these sample letters of theirs? This should lead us into the topic of how we should use our correspondence to develop our friendships with others or to extend ourselves to those who are not near us.

Topic: Why do we correspond with others? In this passage from *Little Women*, we see the girls able to communicate with their mother while she is away taking care of their father who had been injured while serving our country. What other times do we correspond with people?

Answers may vary but when the discussion is lagging, try to suggest some of these. Make sure to have covered all occasions for correspondence before finishing. If you prefer to have a chart ready to refer to, by all means, make one on poster board ahead of time and pull it out now as a visual for the girls.

1. To keep in touch
2. Pen pals
3. Write to inform
4. Thank you for a visit or present
5. Invite to a party
6. Get Well Soon
7. Sympathy for a death in the family
8. For special occasions: birthday, anniversary, Christmas, etc.

The Lesson

Note to Hostess: In the practical today, you will be discussing with the girls how to correspond with another, either in formal notes such as a thank you, or as a personal note of salutations or well being. This lesson and the direction it takes depends largely on your vision for it. It is necessary for this skill to have the correct form for the letter. In the practice, you can decorate the letters to bring in an artistic aspect if you want to. If you are a gifted scrap booker or stamper, etc. you may really open this activity up to be a lot of fun for the girls. It may make the dreaded letter writing a more enjoyable task. Just remember they are learning a skill and may need help in what to say, so please keep posted ideas of things to include in the letter. (No stamping each other, tattoos are not lady-like.)

Things Hostess needs ahead of time: Chalkboard, poster board or white board to demonstrate proper form for a letter. Nice paper or note cards for girls to make notes and envelopes. (If you would rather girls bring their own, then please indicate that to the group ahead of time). Pencils, pens, colored writing instruments, decorative things such as stickers, stamps or other art supplies. (Please stay as simple or fancy as you would like or are gifted to do.) Next, please have index cards for each girl in your group with girls full names including Miss Mary Jones and their addresses written as it should appear on an envelope. Put on bottom, please write to once per week. Include a card for each girl in group and put in basket, bucket, whatever to draw from for pen pals. Finally, you may want to have some special letters of your own on hand either when you were a girl or from the present to show as an example.

Demonstration: Gather the girls at the table where you will be working. Tell the girls that there are times when we need to correspond with others. This is a skill necessary to bring hospitality to others, another way to serve them. There is a special way, a proper way, to do this so each time we write, our notes or letters look pretty and are easy to read. We always want to make sure that when we serve others that we present whatever we are doing in a nice and attractive way. Writing is included in this. It is nothing to be scared of or feel you don't know how to do it. Please stress that this is not schoolwork. No one is grading them on their work. They are just learning how to write a note. **Writing is just talking on paper. Remind them of the passage from *Little Women* when Meg and Jo just told their mother what was happening and what they were thinking.** For girls who like to talk, just write it down. For girls that are shy, this may be an easier way for them to talk with others and a nice way to practice conversation. I am going to teach you the form or framework for your note and you are going to make the painting with words. Let's get started.

Each girl should be seated with a piece of paper and writing utensil. You will have a letter posted so they can see the proper form. Write it on a white board or poster board big enough so everyone can see it. Indenting usually causes the most problems, and then lining the rest of the paragraph up on the left side.

1) Remind the girls that we spoke earlier about different types of correspondence. Today they are going to write a letter "to keep in touch" with someone, perhaps a grandparent or cousin. They could even write to their dad at work so he will get a surprise letter. (They were supposed to bring the name and address.) If they didn't, just think of someone now. Dear....,

2) Things to include in a letter: These are suggestions for the girls when they are trying to think of what to write about. They do not need to talk about all of them but try to include three different subjects to make their letter interesting. (Post this list for the girls to see or have little cards done like a menu and set on each end of table for reference.) Sometimes we all have a tendency of writing such a quick note that we didn't tell the recipient anything about our lives. We greeted them and ended. Let's try to include some of these things:

* Activities you have been doing
* Books you have been reading
* Visitors you have had - for example, if grandparents or other relatives came for a visit
* Artwork of your own or postcards of others'
* Trips you've taken or museums or field trips you've had
* Food or parties you've enjoyed
* Friends or visits they've recently had
* Include artwork, poems, recipes, riddles

3) Present the form of the letter pointing to the parts using these names.

i. The heading
ii. The salutation
iii. The body of the letter
iv. The close
v. The signature

Sample Letter

325 Hospitality Drive
Lake Beautiful, IL 33923
October 7, 2007

Dear Mary,

I am writing you now from my fun hospitality club. We are learning all about how to serve others. Today, of course, we are learning to write letters and to correspond with others.

Did you know that letter writing is just talking on paper? I am so excited because it used to scare me to write letters. I guess that is why it has been so long since you've heard from me; but not anymore. Now that I know the secret, I will write often.

What have you been up to since we last saw you? I remember you said you were going to try out for a play. Did you make it? I hope so. I was in a play last year and I had so much fun. The singing was kind of hard for me but I loved the group dance we got to do in the ball scene. We all got to wear big, fancy dresses. Mine was purple velvet with white lace. My mom said it reminded her of a picture she saw in a Victorian book.

I don't have long to write today but I did want to include the book I was reading. I am in the middle of the Moffat series. Have you ever read them? You should as I think with our common interests that you would like it just as much as I do. It's about a middle-sized family like ours and all the antics and things they like to do. It's very funny and easy to read. I'm almost done with the series. Any suggestions what to read next?

I am enclosing a recipe I think you would like. It is from my cookbook for tea parties. It's called peanut clusters but my dad said they used to make something just like it for Boy Scouts called Gorp. Either way, its easy, I can make it all by myself and everyone loves it. Try it! Now you'll have to write to tell me how you like it.

I must scoot even though I have loads of other things to tell you. Write soon if you can.

Love,
Your cousin, Jenny

4) Once everyone's letters are written, have the girls begin to decorate them with stamps, coloring pencils, etc. Maybe have them set it on a colored piece of paper or use decorative scissors for the edges.

5) Have the girls label the envelopes and fold letter neatly to put in. Have them place this in their binder to mail from home unless you planned on doing this.

Conclusion: Review the seven reasons to correspond with someone. Pick names from the bowl with each girl's name and address and assign pen pals for the month. Ask the girls to write to their pen pals once a week for this month. Put pen pal cards in their binders with their books. End with a prayer.

TAKE HOME: Don't forget to write your pen pal! Mail your letter you wrote at the meeting. Ask your mom for the address and a stamp.

Try some of these activities this month:

* **Look up the Epistles in the New Testament.** Pick a favorite one and copy it for your binder under correspondence. Use a copier and then decorate the edges of the page. Perhaps cut it and mount it on card stock or if you enjoy calligraphy, hand copy it in your best writing. Pay special attention at Mass this week when either Father or the reader says, "a Reading from the Letter of …..to the ..." See the value letters hold. These are over 2000 years old and are still being read and treasured.

* **Pen Pals:** Begin writing with a relative or girl in your group. Try to write once a week for this month and see how it develops. Make it interesting. Please do not write: "I got your letter. It was nice. I am fine. How are you. Write back. From, Mary." There is no information and this is not a proper correspondence. Remember the rules from the skill of what may be included in a note. Remember also that when you receive a letter, it is good manners to write back promptly. If we put it off until later, we often forget to do it. The person you are corresponding with is just as excited about getting a letter as you are. This is a simple way for us to think about others before ourselves. If you don't have time to write, why not send her a bookmark, stickers or something of the like so she has something in her mailbox when the truck arrives. It's like a smile in an envelope.

* **Holiday Notes:** Christmas cards, valentine cards, birthdays, feast days, Thanksgiving, and Easter are all great opportunities and reminders for us to write to people we may not get to see that often or who might enjoy an extra hello. Make sure to always write your grandparents.

* **Library:** Get a book of famous letters out from the library and read some to your family. Copy your favorites to put in your binder. Perhaps a letter written by a founder of our country, a favorite author, or a saint.

* **Diary/Journal:** Begin a personal journal if you haven't already and try to write in it every day. This is a good way to practice writing about things that interest you so you can write better to others. It is also an excellent history for yourself as you get older to see yourself how you have changed or stayed the same. You can also include poetry or favorite stories.

* **Organize a letter writing party** and get a list of names from a local nursing home or list of names of older people in the parish or shut-ins and have all your guests write to them. This idea could also be applied to military away from home any time of year. So many people do things at Christmas for these people mentioned and the rest of the year, everyone forgets them. It would actually be nicer to write them when it isn't a holiday because they may not get any letters.

* **Political Literature:** We can also use our skill of hospitality and correspondence to help our country and issues that are dear to our hearts. If this is a time when a candidate may be running for office who needs our help, maybe you can organize some friends to stuff some envelopes for the candidate or hand the literature out door to door with adult supervision. Remember hospitality is a way to serve others and this candidate is willing to stand up for us and what we believe.

* **Make your own paper:** You'll need two cups shredded newspaper, one piece colored construction paper or two and a half pieces of two different colors, ripped up, one screen in a frame (an old window screen works well). You'll also need a plastic tub large enough to hold the screen, one tablespoon of cornstarch, thread (metallic is nice) flower petals, glitter, or other ornamentation that can go into the paper. Shred paper into six cups of water in large pot. Bring to a boil and break apart newsprint. Boil until paper looks like runny oatmeal. This is the paper slurry. Put slurry in the tub and add three more potfuls of water. Add thread, glitter or petals. Stir up the slurry and put the screen into the tub. Lift out carefully and slowly so that the water runs through the screen and the paper pulp collects on the screen. Place screen on several folded towels. Place a folded towel on top of paper and roll over towel with a rolling pin to squeeze out the excess water. Let dry several hours. Pull paper from edges of screen and finish drying on a flat surface.

FIELD TRIPS:

* **Visit a paper store** - See all the beautiful papers that are available to us now. Perhaps buy some with certain people in mind that we may want to write to. Mom, see if you can arrange perhaps for a class to have some demonstrations on layering and using the papers. Check about fees ahead of time if they offer such a class.

* **Museums:** Visit a museum that has a collection of famous letters. It is wonderful to see how well they have been preserved. Sometimes the writing is hard to read but perhaps you will get lucky and decipher them easily. Also, note at the museum the way that other times and cultures communicated, not just through letters. Hieroglyphics is a wonderful illustration of this. It was hundreds of years before these "letters" could be decoded but look at the history and knowledge it has brought us about a time long ago. A diocesan museum or archives are

always a nice way to find out the history of Catholics in your area. See where the sacraments are recorded and preserved. Motherhouses and religious orders also have their own archives, which may be able to be viewed with prior permission.

Recommended Reading: *Little Women* by Louisa May Alcott is an excellent story showing family life and the virtue of hospitality in many different ways. It shows how to host, how to be a good guest, how to bring hospitality to those in need, how to sacrifice and how to write. If you think it a level too difficult to read yet, get a copy on tape or CD from your library and listen to a little each day (maybe while you're cleaning).

Daddy Long Legs by Jean Webster is a book entirely made up of letters but not as a journal. It is written about a girl who was an orphan but getting too old for the orphanage. She was sponsored by an anonymous benefactor to attend college. A fund was set up for many things including clothing and social events. This benefactor changed her life but his one request was that the main character write to him on a regular basis informing him of the events in her life. He has high aspirations for her to be a writer and the letters will provide practice. It's very whimsical, but fun. The book on tape version is very good and easy to enjoy. This book, outside of highlighting the skill for this month of correspondence, emphasizes the good one can do in being generous to others. Further, the gratitude we should show to those who extend hospitality to us. Watch out for the surprise ending!

Recommended Movies: *Little Women* - There are three great versions, one with Katherine Hepburn and one with June Allyson. The former is black and white and the latter is in color. The third is a modern version that many people enjoy as well. I feel this last version does not stress the femininity of the Little Women and their striving for virtue. Susan Sarandon who plays Marmee in this version, seems to incite her girls to independence in a feminist understanding of the word rather than to become "accomplished" and virtuous young ladies. Yet, I like that they include certain scenes from the book left out in other versions of the film. It is a good opportunity to watch two with your girls and talk about the artistic interpretation the film-makers took in each.

Forms To Remember for Different Types of Correspondence

Types of Correspondence:

1. **To keep in touch**
2. **Pen pals**
3. **Write to inform**
4. **Thank you for a visit or present**
5. **Invite to a party**
6. **Get Well Soon**

7. Sympathy for a death in the family

8. For special occasions: birthday, anniversary, Christmas, etc.

Things you may like to include in a letter:

*   Activities you have been doing
*   Books you have been reading
*   Visitors you have had - for example, if grandparents or other relatives came for a visit
*   Artwork of your own or postcards of others'
*   Trips you've taken or museums or field trips you've had
*   Food or parties you've enjoyed
*   Friends or visits they've recently had
*   Include artwork, poems, recipes, riddles

Sample Friendly Letter used for Keeping in Touch, Pen Pals or To Inform

325 Hospitality Drive
Lake Beautiful, IL 33923
October 7, 2007

Dear Mary,

Well, I am writing you now from my fun hospitality club. We are learning all about how to serve others. Today, of course, we are learning to write letters and to correspond with others.

Did you know that letter writing is just talking on paper? I am so excited because it used to scare me to write letters. I guess that is why it has been so long since you've heard from me; but not anymore. Now that I know the secret, I will write often.

What have you been up to since we last saw you? I remember you said you were going to try out for a play. Did you make it? I hope so. I was in a play last year and I had so much fun. The singing was kind of hard for me, but I loved the group dance we got to do in the ball scene. We all got to wear big, fancy dresses. Mine was purple velvet with white lace. My mom said it reminded her of a picture she saw in a Victorian book.

I don't have long to write today but I did want to include the book I was reading. I am in the middle of the Moffat series. Have you ever read them? You should as I think with our common interests that you would like it just as much as I do. It's about a middle-sized family like ours and all the antics and things they like to do. I'm almost done with the series. Any suggestions what to read next?

I am enclosing a recipe I think you would like. It is from my cookbook for tea parties. It's called peanut clusters but my dad said they used to make something just like it for Boy Scouts called Gorp. Either way, its easy, I can make it all by myself and everyone loves it. Try it! Now you'll have to write to tell me how you like it.

I must scoot even though I have loads of other things to tell you. Write soon if you can.

Love,
Your cousin, Jenny

Sample Thank You Letter

325 Hospitality Drive
Lake Beautiful, IL 33923
October 7, 2007

Dear Mary,

Thank you so much for the wonderful visit at your house. Playing Little Women was certainly a good idea. I hope we can play it again soon. Maybe next time at my house.

I loved the dinner your mom made. Please tell her that pasta is one of my favorite foods and I never had that sauce before. I told my mom all about it. She is anxious to try it herself.

It was very thoughtful to have me over. Thanks again. I wish it didn't have to end.

Your friend,

Thank You for a Present
(Make it interesting - Remember writing is just talking on paper)

325 Hospitality Drive
Lake Beautiful, IL 33923
October 7, 2007

Dear Mary,

Thank you so much for the paper doll set. I tried to make some myself once but they didn't turn out very well so I was truly excited when I unwrapped yours. I am about half-way through cutting out the clothes.

I thought I could use the clothes as a pattern to make some more on some card-stock my mother got for me. I'll let you know how they turn out.

It was really nice of you to remember my birthday. I am really enjoying your present.

Your niece,
Jenny

Sample Letter to Someone who is Sick

325 Hospitality Drive
Lake Beautiful, IL 33923
January 27, 2007

Dear Mary,

I hope this letter finds you better than when we last heard from you. I am so sorry you had to get your tonsils out. At least you got to eat ice cream. I have to wait for Sunday for that!

We sure missed seeing you at the last Hospitality Club but I got you the papers to put in your binder. I will give them to you when I see you.

I have a riddle for you: What is a big dish but you don't eat out of it? This will give you something to think about while you're stuck in bed. I am also sending along one of my favorite movies called *Heidi*. It reminds me of a lot of the things we learned in class and how to be generous to others. Hope you enjoy it.

See you on the road to recovery!

Your friend,
Jenny

P.S. The answer to the riddle is: The Superbowl!

Sample Letter for Sympathy

325 Hospitality Drive
Lake Beautiful, IL 33923
October 7, 2007

Dear Mary,

My mother told me that your grandfather passed away. I am very sorry about that. I remember the stories you told me about him. He seemed like a really nice person. I wish I could have met him.

I will say some prayers for him and hope you are not too sad. Please call me soon so we can visit. You said he always told you that getting together with good friends was a great way to use your time well.

Love,
Jenny

Sample Invitation

You are cordially invited to
A party for my eleventh birthday
On
Saturday, May 5, 2007
At the home of
Jenny Stockum
325 Hospitality Drive
Lake Beautiful, IL 33923

R.S.V.P. before May 1, 2007 at 847.322.3255

Hospitality: The Skill of Bringing Hospitality to Others

"I was sick and you visited me." Matthew 25:36

Holy Inspiration: *The Visitation:* St. Luke tells us that when the archangel, Gabriel, told Mary that Elizabeth, her cousin, was to have a child, she went "in haste to the hill country" where Elizabeth lived. Our Lady did not think of herself in her own time of pregnancy but put another's needs in front of her own. Compassion, thinking of others' pain, is an important part to the virtue of hospitality. Compassion is understanding and feeling others' crosses and difficulties and wanting to ease others' pains by bringing joy to them through our work, friendship, help and love. This is what Mary did for Elizabeth. This is what we want to do for others. The more we become familiar with the life of Our Blessed Mother, the more we will understand how to practice compassion. Compassion is a virtue to be practiced at home as well as in other places. It has to do with how we bring joy to others in times of struggle, discouragement, frustration and pain. Let us pray this month to practice this skill with the love of Our Lady and Lord.

Our Lady's Patronage: To coincide with our "Holy Inspiration," we will put this skill under the patronage of Our Lady of the Visitation. Let us ask Mary's intercession to always put others first and to serve them as we would serve Christ.

Charm: Pineapple

Literature Example: This month we have a passage to discuss relating the virtue of bringing joy to others, in a light-hearted manner, as the girls' efforts did not always go according to plans. This passage is found in a book by Astrid Lindgren called *The Children of Noisy Village* in the chapter titled "Anna and I Make People Happy":

> One day at school Miss Johnson said we should always try to make other people happy. We should never do anything that would make anyone feel bad, she said. Well, that same afternoon Anna and I sat on our back stairs talking, and we decided to start making people happy right away.
>
> The trouble was that we didn't quite know how to go about it. We decided to start with Agda, so we went into the kitchen, where she was scrubbing the floor.
>
> "Agda," I said, "can you tell me something that we could do to make you happy?"
>
> "Yes, if you would get out of the kitchen while I'm scrubbing the floor, I would be very happy," said Agda.
>
> We went outside again. It wasn't much fun to make people happy that way. Anyway, I don't think that's what Miss Johnson meant......*(After trying to make a few more people happy and not having*

it work out.)

So I went back to Anna, and I said that Miss Johnson probably had no idea how hard it was to find someone to make happy.

"I know, let's try Grandfather," Anna said.

So we went to Grandfather's.

"Are my little friends coming to see me?" said Grandfather. "That makes me very happy!"

Wasn't that a shame! We had hardly come inside the door, and Grandfather was already happy. There was nothing left for us to do.

"No, Grandfather," said Anna. "Don't tell us that you're already happy. We want to do something to make you happy. You have to help us think of something, because Miss Johnson says we have to make other people happy."

"You could perhaps read the paper to me. That would make me happy," said Grandfather.

"Well, yes, but we do that so often that there's nothing special about it."

All of a sudden Anna said, "Grandfather, you hardly ever get to leave this room. Wouldn't you be awfully happy if we took you for a walk?"

Grandfather didn't look very happy at the suggestion, but he promised to go with us. Anna and I walked on either side of Grandfather and led him, because he can't see where he's going. We took him all around Noisy Village and talked and told him things the whole time. The wind had started to blow, and it rained a little, but we didn't mind because we were bound and determined to make Grandfather happy.

As we were walking along Grandfather said, "Don't you think we've walked enough now? I'd like to go to bed."

We led Grandfather back to his room. He undressed right away and crept into his bed, although it wasn't night yet. Anna tucked him in. He looked a little tired.

Before we left, Anna said, "Grandfather, what's the nicest thing that's happened to you all day?"

We both thought he'd say that the walk had been the nicest thing. But Grandfather said, "The nicest thing that's happened to me today - well, snuggling down in my nice warm bed. I feel very   tired."

Afterwards, Anna and I had to do our homework so we didn't have time to make any more people happy that day. The next day we still weren't quite sure that we knew the right way to make people happy, so we decided to ask Miss Johnson about it. Miss Johnson said that often very little was needed. You could perhaps sing a song for someone who was sick and alone, or give a flower to someone who never got flowers, or speak kindly to someone who felt bashful and out of place.

Anna and I decided to try again. That afternoon I heard Agda tell Mommy that Karen was sick. She lives by herself in a little house at the edge of the woods. I ran over to Anna right away and said, 'What luck! Karen is sick. Come on, let's go over there and sing to her!'

Karen seemed quite pleased to see us, but she probably wondered why we didn't bring her anything in a basket, because we usually do.

"Do you want us to sing something to you?" I asked.

"Sing?" said Karen, and looked surprised. "Why?"

"To make you happy," said Anna.

"All right, go ahead," said Karen.

We started with "Oh, Susannah," and then we sang "The Farmer in the Dell," all seven verses. Karen didn't look any happier than she had when we started. So then we sang "Little Miss Muffet," and the "The Old Woman Who Lived in a Shoe," and "Mary Had a Little Lamb," and a couple more songs, but Karen still didn't look a bit happier.

Anna and I didn't think it was worth trying any longer, so we said goodbye to Karen.....(They tried several more suggestions, bringing flowers to someone, etc. yet no one seemed happier.)

"Perhaps," I said, "but I've had enough. I'm not going to make any more people happy."

But we did, all the same, because the next day Miss Johnson told us that Martha, a girl in our class, wasn't coming back to school for a long time. She was very, very sick and had to stay in bed several months. That night, before I went to sleep, I lay awake thinking about Martha, and then I decided to give her Bella, my most beautiful doll. This was because I knew that Martha didn't have any toys at all.

In the morning when I told Anna that I was going to give Martha my doll, she went to get her nicest story book. And after school we went over to Martha's house. She was in bed and looked very pale. Never have I seen anyone as happy as Martha was when we put Bella and the little storybook beside her pillow and told her that she could keep them both. My, oh my, how happy she was! She hugged Bella and the story book and laughed and laughed. Then she called her mother to come and see her presents.

When we were outside the door, I said to Anna, "Isn't it funny, now we've made someone happy without even trying."

Discussion: Ask the girls what they learned from this passage about making people happy? This is one of the primary goals of hospitality: to make others happy through serving their needs before our own. How did Anna and Lisa try to do this? Does it sound like something they were already doing before the teacher told them to "make others happy?" Let the girls discuss this. Make sure by the end that if we form ourselves to be in the habit of looking to others, we will not have to try so hard. We will bring others joy just through friendship, as these girls did at the end. They didn't set out to make Martha happy at the end. Lisa and Anna were already in the habit of helping others and so when they heard that she was sick, they couldn't stop thinking of her.

This is true compassion. What did they bring to her? They thought of their favorite thing they owned and gave it to her. When we give truly from our heart, the joy always comes.

Look at the other instances in the story of bringing joy to others. Why weren't the people made happy? (Because they weren't looking at what would make the other person happy. They were doing things that they were told would make some people happy.) We have to look to the person themselves whom we are helping. Grandpa loved just having them visit and read to him. So, even if it didn't seem exciting to the girls, it was what he wanted.

Often when we have friends for a visit, we want to be good hostesses. The best way is to prepare a game that you know they would enjoy, based on their interests. It may not be what you would want but we are not serving ourselves. This is what the story is trying to teach us about bringing hospitality to others. It can be in our home or at another's. The virtue lies in how we bring the joy or compassion not in where we do it. It is through our friendship and seeking each other's needs that we will form the habit.

The Lesson

Notes to the Hostess: This is a very important lesson to teach the girls this month. It is not as much about a skill as it is about understanding when and where to practice this virtue of hospitality. Thus far, they have been learning particular skills related to the practical aspect of the virtue, but this month is about putting it into practice. They will use many of their learned skills to bring hospitality to others: cooking, cleaning, table setting, conversation, love of literature and so forth. Many of these will be their tools to share happiness with others. Today will be a little different from the other months, as it will be a brain storm session for the girls to look at their own lives, and make a list of other people they can help and what they can do or bring to them. As always, practice is important in formation. The activity today is playing games, a way for the girls to grow in their friendships, manners, and looking out for each other.

Things the Hostess Needs: Paper and pencils for the girls, games for activity

Practice: Have the girls sit in a comfortable area where they can write and have them divide their paper into four columns: Who, When, Why and What. You will be discussing the possibilities of who you would bring hospitality to, when you would do it and why. They will write in their lists answers that apply to people and circumstances in their own lives. I will give a list below but by all means, let the girls build their lists together. The youth, as you see in the story, often surpass ideas we can come up with. They will keep these lists in their binders to refer to for Take Home.

Who: Someone in need at the parish: a priest, a grandparent, a relative, a friend, a neighbor, a nursing home who welcomes visitors, moms with small kids or moms with children with disabilities.

When should we bring hospitality to others: Everyday. We can bring it to those we meet each day at home or at sports, in our parishes, classes, or in others' homes. Sometimes there are occasions to try even harder for someone like their birthdays or special occasions such as a day a friend or sibling receives a sacrament for the first time. We must on these occasions think of the other in a different way. We must be happy for others in their celebrations and forget about our own needs and wants at these times.

Why should we bring hospitality to others: Someone is sick, had a new baby, live alone, are disabled, sad, or just to surprise them. (Often we don't know always when someone needs a bit of cheer. If we make a habit of asking our angels in the morning prayer time to guide us to those who need us, they will without our even knowing it.)

What to do: This can be as simple as bringing a new game to someone and teaching it to them, or playing a game with a younger sibling or someone who doesn't have someone to play with them. It can just be doing something special for someone like leaving them a note or a book they'd enjoy, doing someone's job for them or repairing something of theirs that is broken.

Using these guidelines, help the girls particularize their lists. Who in their lives can they bring hospitality to?

Stories: When the girls are done with their lists have them put them in their binders with their companion book. Now look ahead at the Take Home page for this month. There are some lovely stories you could share with the girls about the history of the St. Joseph Table (see story following page), about the pineapple as the symbol of hospitality, or about St. Frances of Rome, a model of bringing hospitality to others. These are important and inspirational stories for the girls. They will help them understand what we have been talking about. Tell them when you're finished that they are in their TAKE HOME if they want to share these stories with their family.

Spend the remainder of the time playing games to encourage friendship and good manners among the girls.

Games: Musical Chairs, board games and team games like charades. By all means, use a game you know well that would work for a big group. These are only suggestions. Have fun with this part.

Conclusion: Remind the girls to practice their lists this month. Ask Our Lady and St. Elizabeth to help us bring hospitality to others. Playing games and including others can be simple ways to bring hospitality to others as well as practicing the corporal works of mercy like visiting the sick. March is the month that is a part of Lent which is a great time to practice bringing hospitality to others. Look to St. Joseph and St. Patrick whose feast days we celebrate this month, and note how they brought our Faith to others through their own hospitality. St. Patrick and St. Joseph, pray for us!

TAKE HOME: Don't forget your list you made at the meeting. Try to help some of the people on it.

* **Plan a St. Joseph's Table or attend one.** This history of the St. Joseph Table is one of doing for others. According to legend, there was a famine in Sicily many centuries ago. The villagers prayed to St. Joseph and asked him to intercede for them. The famine ended as God answered their pleas. They celebrated with a special feast of thanksgiving which was held in commemoration of Saint Joseph. This celebration became tradition. Wealthy families prepared huge buffets of food and invited the less fortunate people of the village, especially the homeless and sick, to partake. Every March 19th, the feast of St. Joseph, this tradition continues all over the world. As it started in Italy, the foods at the table are Italian. Red tablecloths can be laid as the base and many times there are statues of the saint placed at the center. The menu can be as simple as meatball sandwiches with Italian cookies for dessert or as elaborate as you choose to get. It is the idea we want to practice and the tradition not the extravagance.

* **March19th:** Pack an Italian basket and bring it to someone. Put in a package of dried pasta, a jar of marinara, a loaf of crusty bread, a prayer to St. Joseph and some cookies. Line the basket with a piece of red and white cloth and a note saying you hope they will enjoy their own St. Joseph Table at home. This may even be a tradition your family may want to start, bringing these baskets to several families to enjoy or to a person you know is so busy that they can never cook a meal. Have Fun!

* Take out list you made at meeting and try to do some of these means of hospitality.

* **Basket Ideas:** Try one of these ways to bring hospitality to another.

1) **For a lonely person or a sick friend:** Pack a basket with a good book, a good movie, a nice note and a book of puzzles.

2) **A hostess present:** a nice soap or hand lotion, or some note cards tied with a bow.

3) **A new Mom:** A pot of soup (minestrone or potato are easy) and some bread. Sew a little baby blanket with some fleece or make a tie blanket. (The fabric stores have easy directions. All you need are two pieces of fleece the same size and a pair of scissors.)

4) **A teacher or coach:** Use the Italian basket idea above but make a colander be your basket which they can use to drain their pasta.

* **Baskets of Your Time:** Look at your list you made at Little Women Club and see if there are things or people you came up with that you can do some-

thing for. Remember from our story that bringing 'things' to others is often not what they need. Maybe someone just enjoys your company. Play a game or read to someone who is bed-ridden or alone. The corporal works of mercy are a great list of ideas and ways to bring hospitality to others. Pray about these and see what happens.

*   Read a book, (a simple one by Father Lovasik is easily available) on the Seven Corporal Works of Mercy, which are:

Feed the hungry
Give drink to the thirsty
Welcome the stranger
Clothe the naked
Visit the sick
Visit the prisoner
Bury the dead

*   **The Pineapple:** A fun gift is to bring someone a pineapple with a card that you prepare explaining its symbolism of hospitality. It will show your hostess or friend how much you appreciate their hospitality towards you. Make a few copies and keep them in this section of your binder always ready when you need them. Just print on some card stock, punch a hole and tie with a ribbon around the top of the pineapple.

THE PINEAPPLE STORY: Years ago, Christopher Columbus brought this fruit back to Europe from the Caribbean Islands. It was expensive at the time since fresh fruit was rare. Yet, it still became very popular among Europeans and, later, those in the American colonies. In those times, hospitality - welcoming others into ones' lives and homes - was a central virtue to practice. The pineapple became the central symbol of this hospitality as hostesses often used it as the centerpiece and food of a party given in a certain person's honor. As the fruit was rare and expensive, it showed to the guest that only the best would due for their visit. The pineapple continued to become the symbol of welcome, good cheer, graciousness, warmth and conviviality, all parts of the virtue of hospitality. Sailors even began to post a pineapple at their door after a long journey to show others that they had returned and that all were welcome.

*   Read a biography on St. Frances of Rome - She is a wonderful patron of hospitality as she brought food to the poor and started a home for orphans. She was very wealthy but still sacrificed by wearing a hair shirt which is very uncomfortable under her beautiful silks and velvets that she was required to wear because of her state in life.

FIELD TRIPS:

*   Attend a St. Joseph's Table at your parish or other place.

Recommended Reading: *The Children of Noisy Village* by Astrid Lindgren

Hospitality: The Skill of Sewing and Dressing Modestly

"Commit everything to the Lord. Trust Him to help you and He will."
Psalm 37:5

Holy Inspiration: St. Anne and Our Lady must have worked very hard preparing with detail and diligence the garments that would become our Lord's first clothes. With each stitch, each woman thought of the Messiah that would come to save the world from sin, and how his sweet little hands would hold theirs so tenderly. Love and skill are what went into those beautiful baby clothes and love and skill are what we can use to make lovely things for others. Just as thoughts of our Savior went into the detailed work of His garments, so too should we turn the details of our work into prayers or sacrifices for Our Lord. Everything we do, whether it is school work, dishes, games or play can all be and should be a prayer. We can lift these things of everyday life to a supernatural level by offering our day every morning to the Sacred Heart. St. Anne, pray for us. Our Lady, Mother of Our Lord, pray for us.

Our Lady's Patronage: One can just picture the grandmother of Christ passing on the skill of sewing onto Our Lady. This is such a special mother/daughter time that we ask Our Lady, daughter of St. Anne, for her special prayers as our daughters learn this skill from their mothers. And, in accordance with our "Holy Inspiration," ask St. Anne for her blessings while we practice this skill.

Charm: Sewing Machine

Literature Example: In the following passage from *Jo's Boys*, the March girls are grown with homes of their own. Yet, they feel strongly the need for a time and place for everything, especially their sewing. Sewing to them is not just a skill, a necessity for a well-formed "little woman," but can become a means of hospitality as you shall see. Enjoy!

>   Among the various customs which had very naturally sprung up was one especially useful and interesting to "the girls" as the young women liked to be called. It all grew out of the old sewing hour still kept up by the three sisters long after the little work-boxes had expanded into big baskets full of household mending. They were busy women, yet on Saturdays they tried to meet in one of the three sewing rooms, for even classic Parnassus had its nook where Mrs. Amy often sat among her servants, teaching them to make and mend, thereby giving them a respect for economy, since the rich lady did not scorn to darn her hose or sew on buttons. In these household retreats, with books and work, and their daughters by them, they read, and sewed, and talked in the sweetest pri-

vacy that domestic women love, and can make so helpful by a wise mixture of cooks and chemistry, table linen and theology, prosaic duties and good poetry.

Mrs. Meg was the first to propose enlarging this little circle, for as she went her motherly rounds among the young women, she found a sad lack of order, skill, and industry in this branch of education. Latin, Greek, the higher mathematics, and science of all sorts prospered finely, but dust gathered on the work-baskets, frayed elbows went unheeded, and some of the blue stockings sadly needed mending. Anxious lest the usual sneer at learned women should apply to 'our girls,' she gently lured two or three of the most untidy to her house and made the hour so pleasant, the lesson so kindly, that they took the hint, were grateful for the favor, and asked to come again. Others begged to make the detested weekly duty lighter by joining the party, and soon it was a privilege so desired that the old museum was refitted with sewing machines, tables, rocking chairs, and a cheerful fireplace, so that, rain or shine, the needles might go on undisturbed.

Discussion: How did you enjoy this passage? How does it apply to our skill at hand, how is sewing a means of hospitality? Note to the hostess: See if the girls notice in the passage that they girls are not just learning and using the skill itself to show hospitality for their families, but they use the time in which they practice the skill, to extend their knowledge and love to girls who have not been as fortunate as they have. This is an important point, although we are learning these skills as part of a practice of hospitality, sometimes the time in which we practice the skills themselves can lend an opportunity to extend a thoughtful ear and teaching moment to another. We should always be on guard to look for these opportunities.

The Lesson

Notes to the Hostess: The bulk of today's lesson will be hands-on, so plan accordingly. Today the girls will be making their "hospitality" aprons. Often in history, women have put on aprons to clean house as well as cook. We see this often in Jane Austen books and movies, *Little House on the Prairie* or others - the apron is a practical way to keep one's clothes clean and tidy. It also symbolizes the care and respect we take of the things we have. Often, we take things for granted, especially clothing. We want the girls to learn to respect their belongings by taking caring of them. By putting on the apron, it also puts on a mind set to work diligently. It is a reminder of the work we are undertaking for ourselves and those for whom we are doing it. This is a simple sewing project and will be a lot of fun to see all the different fabrics everyone has chosen. A picture would be cute at the end with everyone wearing their aprons.

Ahead of time, make certain each girl brings materials needed for apron. This should have been noted at the last meeting but if it was overlooked, notify everyone of the needed materials. Remind the girls by email to bring two pieces of fabric as you will be sewing the apron "pillowcase" style. They may choose a front and plain back or two totally different fabrics for a two-sided apron. They should remember ribbon for apron & thread to match, and scissors. You will want to enlist the assistance of as many moms or older teens who know how to sew straight lines, and borrow as many portable sewing machines as possible. Email your group a couple of times requesting volunteers and machines. You need to set up a sewing area with tables, machines, ironing board and iron, and remember either electrical outlets or extension cords. Check the number of prongs on extension cords to make certain you have the correct kind. Kitchen tables or dining room tables would be ideal for this project but folding tables often used in school rooms can also easily facilitate this project.

Things Hostess Needs: Basic color threads for those who forgot, a couple extra yards of fabric with ribbons for those who forget, lots of straight pins, chalk, rulers/ yardsticks, sewing scissors, iron and ironing board, tables for sewing and chairs. Make your cardboard template triangles 7 x 12, a few of them, for the corner of the aprons. Have some scrap material available for practicing when the girls are first learning before they use the machines. Don't forget a camera for the picture at the end (digital or disposable).

Demonstration:
1.   Show the girls how to thread a machine. Show them what all the sewing machine knobs and buttons are for. Show them how to pull the thread through with the bobbin as well as how to thread a bobbin. Explain about tension in the thread and how to adjust it. Sometimes if the tension is off, the thread will gather in the stitch.

2. Take a scrap fabric and fold to demonstrate how to sew a straight line. Inform the girls that beginners should be sure to go slowly and watch where their hands are. You don't want the needles to sew your hands.

3. Show them how to adjust the placement of the needle or look of the stitch: use a zig zag seam as a sample. (This may be one they will want to use to sew their ribbon on their aprons.)

4. Sewing the Apron - **a)**Take two pieces of cloth 32 inches by 20 inches and show how you will sew the apron. Face the two right sides together and pin. **b)**Then place your cardboard template, explained below, on the top corners of the material. Chalk off the corners. The basic idea is to cut the top corners off the rectangle to create the bib of the apron. Measure 7 inches in from each corner for your top cut and 12 inches down for your waist-line cut. *(A good idea would be to create ahead of time 7 x 12 inch cardboard template triangles for this corner that the girls could lay on the material to cut against or chalk off the corners and then cut. **c)** Next, two 15-inch ribbons will be used, one on each side of the top of the bib. These will be sewn on with a zig zag or straight seam to create the tie of the ribbon around one's neck after the basic part of the apron is sewn. The other ribbon pieces, 24 inches in length each, will be sewn at the edge of the waist, just where the bib ends, to create the ties of the apron around the waist. These will be pinned in at the waist before the initial sewing. (Options: If someone's ribbon is long enough, they can choose to sew it across the entire front of their apron with the zig-zag.) **d)** Once this is done, place the longer ribbons in at the waist , inside between the two fabrics. Pin just the edge of the ribbons into the waist. Make sure the rest of the ribbons are pushed deep towards the center so they don't get caught in the seam as you sew. Now, show how you sew the edges all the way around leaving an opening at the neck. Begin at the top, go down towards the waist, around the bottom and back up the other side, ending again at the neck. **e)** Take out your pins and invert the entire apron through the hole at the neck. Notice the diagram to see where to cut edges and sew ribbons. **f)** Now iron all seams flat, fold under the neck edge, pin in the edge of the neck ribbon and topstitch, even zigzag the neck. It may seem like a few steps but the girls have no problem at all with this. Their aprons will turn out so cute and the different fabrics everyone picks makes it a fun time for them to enjoy each other.

5. Explain to the girls that it is generally a good idea to wash fabric and iron it before sewing with it because it will often shrink in the first washing so you don't want to measure the fabric for cutting until after it has done this first shrinking.

Practice:

1. Ask girls one by one to practice threading machine and sewing seams on scrap material. Once they have a good understanding and can work the machine, proceed to cutting out their aprons. (If there are several machines and moms to help who know how to teach this, by all means, have more than one machine going at a time with the girls not actually doing the sewing, watching carefully.)

2. Have all the girls lay out their material on the floor as you showed them with right sides facing together and pin. Make sure it is flat or the measurements will be off. With chalk and ruler or yard stick, help girls measure off the appropriate sections or use cardboard templates and draw line for angle with chalk to make a clear line for girls to cut. You can also use the edge of yardstick or ruler for hard edge to draw the hypotenuse of the triangle. This is where other moms helping supervise will be invaluable so the girls do not cut in the wrong place and ruin their material.

3. Once all the girls have drawn their lines with chalk, instruct one by one to cut the line they created on both sides of the top of the rectangle. Make sure the girls hold the fabric flat as they cut.

4. Make sure and measure the ribbons and cut those accordingly as well. Pin them in carefully at the waist and make certain they use the longer ribbons here. Now you're ready to make some aprons! Begin sewing aprons. Step by step, sew as you sewed yours in the demonstration.

5. Help the girls sew, invert, and iron their seams. Fold once and again to have a finished edge. Iron all the seams at the same time. Help all to complete this step before sewing the tops and final parts of the aprons. When everyone's seams are ironed, turn off the iron and put it out of the way so no one gets burned.

6. Lastly after all seams are sewn, sew on ribbons and everyone can try theirs on. Voila! The Little Women are ready to practice hospitality: cleaning, cooking, preparing rooms, whatever is needed.

7. Take a picture of all the girls with digital camera to email to all for their binders or with a disposable camera. If using the latter, shoot the entire camera and then everyone will get a photo at the next meeting without need for reprints. The girls can mount it on cardstock and have everyone sign around the picture as a memento of their group. Then slide the card into their sewing section of their binder.

Concluding Discussion: Note that their new skill can be used in making things for others, but can be a means to the practice of modesty, an inherent virtue of all "little women". Modest clothes are often hard to find and a good seamstress can make her own. If any of the girls are interested in sewing and enjoy it, perhaps they can take further classes. They could form a sewing club and practice together as they make some pieces to wear. Many fashions today are very offensive to the dignity of ladies, revealing too much, but also in their lack of classic style. In order to make ourselves available to practice hospitality for others, we need to make ourselves attractive and modest, not in a vain sense, but in a manner conducive to becoming ladies. Sometimes many people think that modesty and fashion can not go together. Christianity has to be attractive so if you want to be a messenger, then your appearance needs to be attractive.

Modesty is not just about being covered but about what to wear and when. Certain occasions call for certain kinds of fashion and we must try to dress for the occasion. To be a good guest or good hostess, we should try to dress fittingly for the event. If we are playing at the park, wearing a skirt might not be modest or appropriate because of climbing, running and all the fun things you like to do at a park. Wearing pants, capris or shorts might be better....but, if you are going to a party, wearing a dress or skirt would be lovely. Shorts would convey to your hostess that you don't appreciate the efforts she/he put forward in having you to their party because you can't even take the time to dress up. The best rule of thumb is to find out what you will be doing at your destination, and dress in a way that befits the activity.

Dressing is not the only part of modesty. The way in which we speak, act or even sit are also an important part of this virtue. Girls especially need to make sure that they don't participate in discussions or use words that Our Blessed Lady would not have used. You must also be aware of how you are sitting. You don't lounge across someone's chair or couch, etc. Young ladies should always keep their knees together, especially when wearing a skirt. Let us conclude today as we pray for our new skill of sewing that we may practice it in our striving to acquire the virtue of hospitality. Let us also pray that we may strive for purity in our modesty of dress, speech and actions. A good practice to start is to say three Hail Marys every night before you go to bed for the virtue of purity. Let us say ours now: Recite three Hail Marys to close.

TAKE HOME:

* Plan a fashion show with your friends. See if you can even get their moms to participate. Give each girl an assigned occasion and have them bring outfits that would represent how to dress modestly and appropriately for that occasion. Pick out a spot in your house where everyone can sit, perhaps set up some chairs where the girls can walk in and out in their outfits. Pick some fun and modest music for the girls to walk to. End with cookies and tea or lemonade.

* Sew a gift for a friend. You could make a handkerchief or napkins for tea time, with ribbon and a little note.

* Make a memory pillow or quilt for yourself to practice your new skill. Take swatches from old dresses of yours, old blankets of yours, toddler memories, etc. Cut fabric into neat and even squares and sew together to make front of pillow or blanket. Get a solid piece of material for back and stuff for pillow or sew blanket pieces inside out leaving room at bottom to invert to right sides for final stitching. This will make a fun history of your life like in the book *The Rag Coat*. You have a bunch of different parts of your life put together in this pillow or quilt.

* Help your mom sew some new curtains maybe she has been wanting to make for a while. It is just a simple rectangle with the edges turned for a finished edge like your aprons. Then use curtain clips to attach to rod. Voila! Some very nice new curtains to finish a room and bring warmth to it. (Maybe surprise her and make some special curtains to be used only at a certain time of year like Christmas curtains.)

* Help a little sister make some doll clothes for her doll or sew a blanket or pillow for her doll. A sleeping bag would also be an easy idea practicing your straight seams. Always ask your mom before cutting any fabric.

* Begin your practice of three Hail Marys at night for purity and modesty in dress, action and thoughts.

Field Trip Options:

* **Museum Quilt Exhibit -** Often museums have a special exhibit on quilts. This would be a wonderful thing for girls to see all the different patterns and quilts that women in history have done and what the patterns stand for. These were often the gifts they gave for weddings, babies and house warmings. The love and skill that went into these quilts is worth the trip to see them.

Recommended Reading: *Jo's Boys* by Louisa May Alcott, Little House Series by Laura Ingalls Wilder. Ma is always sewing shirts by hand and teaching her girls this necessary skill.

Making Your Own Apron

STEP 1:

Cut two 32-inch by 20-inch rectangles of fabric.
Cut two 24-inch waist ribbons.
Cut two 15-inch neck ribbons.

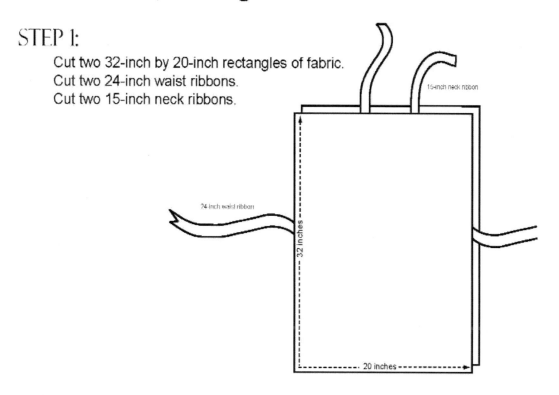

STEP 2:

Chalk off two triangles in the corners of the rectangles just cut by the neck.

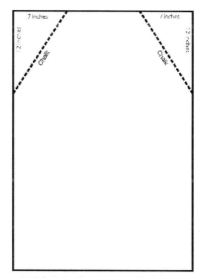

Mark both pieces of fabric.

STEP 3:

Cut off the corners along the chalk lines on both pieces of fabric.

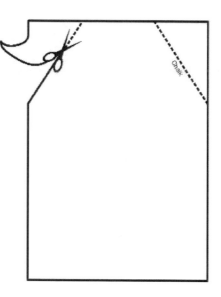

STEP 4:

Place fabric right sides together and pin. Leave the neck open.

Insert waist ribbons into the sides and pin in place. The ends should be inserted between the pieces of fabric and the entire ribbon placed flat within the fabric pieces. Be sure the ribbons do not lie close to the edges of the fabric.

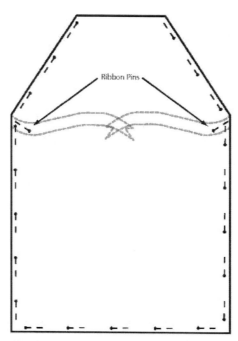

The printed side of the fabric should be on the inside. Only the back sides should show.

STEP 5:

Starting at the neck, sew a 1/4 inch seam around the apron being sure to leave the neck completely open.

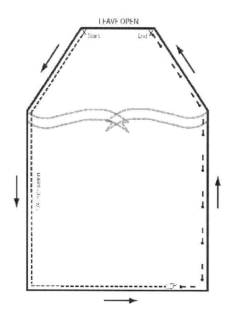

STEP 6:

Turn the apron right side out using the neck opening.

Reach inside, grab the fabric, and turn it right side out as if it was a pillowcase.

Still Open

STEP 7:

Fold the neck into the apron to create a 1/2 inch inseam. Place the ends of the neck ribbons inside the apron at either end of the neck opening. Pin the opening closed, being sure to secure the ribbons.

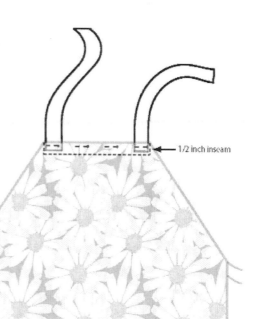

1/2 inch inseam

STEP 8:

Sew a 1/4 inch seam across the neck closing the apron and securing the ribbons.

Sew

Congratulations, you did it!

Hospitality: The Skill of Planning and Preparing a Party

"Let brotherly love continue. Be not forgetful to entertain strangers: for thereby some have entertained angels unaware." Hebrews 13:1-2

Holy Inspiration: *The Wedding Feast at Cana:* Our Lord's first miracle and entrance into public life was at a wedding, a party, celebrating the new marriage of a young couple who were friends of the Holy Family. The couple invited those whom they knew, decided what would be served, who would serve it, and included special foods and drink to celebrate their new marriage. Our Lady noticed that the wine was running low, a celebratory drink for such an occasion. In her compassion for the couple, she did not want them to be embarrassed that they ran out before the celebration was over. It was such an important day for them, the day that would begin their new life together. So, Our Lord, upon request of His dear Mother, asked the stewards to bring in six stone jars full of water. These he changed into the finest wine the guests had ever tasted. This is a good example to us to include Our Lady and Lord in all the events of our lives. If we trust, our own jars will be filled with His grace to go on and do our best. Let us ask our Our Lady and Lord to help us when we prepare for others, to think of the details that will make all feel welcome, and to remember to always be good and generous guests when others welcome us.

Our Lady's Patronage: Our Lady of Perpetual Help will be our intercessor for planning a party. Sometimes when we are in the midst of the planning, our "to do" list may seem overwhelming. We take our eyes off the purpose of the gathering when we get bogged down in the details. We need to ask Our Lady's intercession to gain the correct perspective and to do all our preparations with joy and service to others in mind.

Charm: Tea Cup

Literature Example: In this months literature example, we will look at a passage from one of Louisa May Alcott's lesser known books called: *Aunt Jo's Scrap Bag*. The chapter we want to read entitled "A Happy Birthday" is about a memorable day when a family prepared and planned a special day for their mother/grandmother, a woman who has helped others with her charity for years never wanting anything in return. It reminds us of the importance of celebrating with family and friends and to prepare special things that will please the receiver, not to do necessarily what will please us.

> A certain fine old lady was seventy-three on the eighth of October. The day was always celebrated with splendor by her children and grandchildren; but on this occasion they felt that something unusually interesting and festive should be done, because grandma had lately been

so very ill that no one thought she would ever see another birthday. It pleased God to spare her, however, and here she was, almost as well and gay as ever.

Some families do not celebrate these days and so miss a great deal of pleasure, I think. But the people of whom I write always made a great deal of such occasions and often got up very funny amusements as you shall see.

As grandma was not very strong, some quiet fun must be devised this time and the surprises sprinkled along through the day, lest they should be too much for her if they all burst upon her at once...........

A fine dinner was cooked, and grandma's favorite niece came to it with her, bringing a bag full of goodies and a heart full of love and kind wishes to the old lady.

All the afternoon friends and presents kept coming, and Madam, in her best gown and most imposing cap, sat in state to receive them. A poet came with some lovely flowers; the doctor brought a fine picture; one neighbor sent her a basket of grapes; another took her for a drive; and some poor children, whom grandma had clothed and helped, sent her some nuts they had picked all themselves, while their grateful mother brought a bottle of cream and a dozen eggs.

It was very pleasant, and the bright autumn day was a little harvest time for the old lady, who had sowed the love and charity broadcast with no thought of any reward.

The tea table was ornamented with a splendid cake, white as snow outside but rich and plumy inside, with a gay posy stuck atop of the little Mont Blanc. Mrs. Trot, the housekeeper, made and presented it, and it was so pretty all voted not to cut it until evening, for the table was full of other good things.

...........(After many skits and amusements) It really was a fine sight, I assure you, and grandma was quite overcome by the spectacle. So she was introduced to her gifts as quickly as possible, to divert her mind from the tender thought that all these fond and foolish adornments were to please her....

Discussion: How did the girls like the passage? What did they notice about the characters involved, their virtues and dispositions towards one another? Who were they thinking about? Let us focus on the fact that a party has been planned for a wonderful woman who has done much charity for others in her life without seeking any reward. Birthdays, as the author states, are occasions for celebrating people's lives. We prepare parties not just for birthdays but many occasions to celebrate people's lives, our Faith and Feasts, Friendship and so much more. Each time we plan a celebration, we want to think about the people we are doing it for. What would they like? This is a way we can show our love for one another. Of course, it is a very fun way but it is a lot of work to prepare and plan. We want to remember why we are doing it and who it is for. In this story, we are taught not just to do things out of love but also respect. In today's society, respect for the elderly is a virtue that is sorely lacking. Let us use this passage as an inspiration for our little women and beautiful illustration on how we should treat the elderly in our lives or around us and to show gratitude for what they have done. This is integral to the virtue of hospitality, not just to make others feel welcome and respected but to extend our gratitude for what they have done for us.

This is a lovely set up for today's planning for our moms, to show them how grateful we are for what they have done for us, especially since the grandma in the passage was based on Louisa May Alcott's own mother.

You may ask the girls if they have ever been to a party that was fun to go to? Why? This will help to think about planning a party themselves and what they would include to make their guests feel welcome.

The Lesson

*This lesson would be easiest taught at the mother's house who is hosting the Mother's Day tea but not necessary. *

Notes to the Hostess: Today we will be preparing and planning for the Mother's Tea Party. If this is done in May, it can be a Mother's Day tea party. We will be teaching how to plan a party while actually preparing for this tea. You will have to coordinate with the Mom hosting the tea if it is not you to pass along ahead of time any items prepared today. Please prepare the list or cards of assigned recipes for the girls to take home. If you are hosting and will be using any silver, have the girls learn polishing while polishing yours for the tea. Please also note the size of your group to determine if the recipe amounts will be enough. They have been planned for a group of about 15-18 moms. If more is needed just give some recipes to more than one girl instead of expanding the menu. **Please see the bottom note to hostess of tea and pass along the notes, games, party favors and place cards and anything else to her including menu for her to have for the party. Don't forget to return her silver!**

Things Hostess Needs: Cards or cardstock and writing utensils for invitations, sachet materials (square cloth such as calico and bag of potpourri with thin ribbon), cardstock and hole punch for placecards, decorative scissors and things to decorate place cards and invitations. Have place cards pre-cut to about 1 ½-2 inches by 3 inches in size to make assembling easier. You will need some objects like pineapples or something like them to show how to arrange on a long table. You will need the supplies for the two relay games to practice, including: marble stones, two pairs of high heels, a box for a jewelry box and bowl for stones, two sets of white gloves, two hats, two scarves or boas and other add-ons for the tea party dress up game. You will need silver polish cream and silver pieces to polish (best to call the mom hosting tea for hers to clean: teapot, creamer, sugar bowl, platter).

Demonstration: The best way to prepare for a party is to have a booklet or notebook for parties. You can have a party binder just like your hospitality binder so you will have all your menus, guest lists and recipes in one central place. This helps so you don't have to scramble around with different books especially for recipes. Copy any recipes to include in the one central binder. As time goes by, you will be able to remember who came to what party and what you ate so you don't repeat it the next time. It also saves time on planning food as you already have a list of good "party" food. Another fun idea is to have a "guest book" that your guests sign each time they visit. It makes a wonderful memory of your nice visits and friendships over the years.

Explain the Steps to Planning a Party or Get-Together:

1.   What is the occasion or theme of the party? Write it at top of page so everything will relate to it.

2.   Who will be invited? How many people can you invite? Make a list of the guests and send out invitations. Include a r.s.v.p. with your phone number so you will know who and how many people will be coming. For more casual company, you can invite them over the phone.

3.   What will be served? Try to plan a menu to make ahead of time and decide what plates each item will go on. Use a post-it note to mark the plate. It is easier to plate food for a party. You pick up the plate, see the note, and know exactly what goes on it. This is a time saver later. It also allows time to prepare any silver or other dishes that need cleaning or dusting.

4.   Where and how will it be served? Will it be sit down or buffet? This is partly determined by how many people you will have and what kind of party. If you plan a dinner party, then you will probably limit your guest list. If you have appetizers, you can have more people and have a buffet because people can stand and visit while they eat. If it is a tea or breakfast, you can stand or eat depending on how many people you want to have. Buffets are an easy way for you to entertain as you can lay out the food and people can help themselves and you can visit. The downside is that you can't limit what people take so you have to make sure and have extra. Once you decide where it will be served, pull out tablecloths or napkins and other linens that you will need for the party in order to prepare them. Remember, you don't want to leave anything until the last minute. You will not be serving others well if you are tired and worn out. It is fun when you leave plenty of time to prepare dishes, linens and food at a normal pace.

5.   When will the party be? This will be determined by your theme or food. The time of day will determine your food if by chance the time is the most important aspect.

6.   What games or activities will you have to make the guests feel comfortable or for fun? Plan a couple of games for every party unless it's a dinner party so there is something to do if everyone does not seem to be visiting well. Remember your role in hospitality is to make your guests comfortable.

7.   What will be the decorations? The table settings? The centerpiece? The place cards or seating arrangement?

8. Will there be any party favors?

Practice:

Today we will be preparing for the Mothers' Day Tea as a way to practice our new skill. You will all be giving the tea and serving it for your moms. This will be the day to practice all our skills: setting the table, serving, table manners, clearing a table, cleaning, cooking, good conversation, dressing appropriately and all the parts that make up the virtue of hospitality. What a wonderful person to serve: your mom.

1.   Make invitations for Moms: This can be handwritten on cardstock and decorated, or on the computer ahead of time, and you can have the girls cut and mount it on a doily and cardstock. Or you can buy invitations and they can fill them in. It would be wonderful to have stickers or cards printed with pineapples on them, the symbol for hospitality. Have the information written where the girls can copy it.

You are cordially invited to a Mother's Day Tea prepared in your honor.

On

Day, Date

At

Place

Given By

The Little Women Hospitality Club

*Please bring your favorite tea cup and a baby picture with your name on the back

RSVP To Hostess Name and Phone Number

Note Moms bringing tea cups - Often moms don't get an opportunity to share their good china or use that special pattern they so carefully picked out when they were married. This is a fun way for them to showcase their china which reflects their personality and taste. It's a great conversation starter to get the party going.

The Baby Pictures - These you will set in a special place, a side table, a large tray or frame with numbers under each picture. Each guest will be given a printed list of all the moms and will place the number of the picture next to the name of the baby they think it is. The mom who guesses the most wins.

2.   Make Place Cards for Tea - This will combine place cards and party favors in one. Give each girl a square of calico, some ribbon and some potpourri. Show them how to make sachets and have each girl make one. Next, make little name cards. Give each girl a small rectangle of cardstock for the name card. They will make a hole punch in the corner, write their mom's name on it and tie it to the ribbon on the sachet so the name is facing out. You can use decorative scissors to shape the edges of the card. Direct the girls to collect these into a shoe box or similar item for safekeeping for the party.

3. **Plan your menu** - Start by explaining the types of food a tea would have: finger sandwiches, small sweets and breads and tea and coffee. For girls, a cold drink is also nice to have such as a sparkling juice. Remember the small things such as sugar cubes, cream for the tea, and butter and jams or curds for the breads. Build the list with the girls so they see the process. Explain that they want to pick things easy to make that can be done ahead for any party. Use poster board, chalkboard or the like so all the girls can see. When this process is done, show them the menu planned for the tea. Ask each girl to pick an item from the list to make herself at home and bring to the tea on a special plate. (All the recipes have been tested with children and are easy to make.) Tell them before they plate their food to bring to the tea, be sure to mark the bottom of the plate with a piece of masking tape with their name. Then they won't lose their plate and if they forget to take it home, the hostess knows who it belongs to. Hand the girls the card with the recipe they chose to put in their binder to have for the party. They are also listed in their companion books if they want to circle the one they chose. Please keep a list of who got assigned what dish and save for hosting mom. Maybe someone could email a reminder to each girl so the moms know what their daughters volunteered to bring.

4. **Printing the menu for guests** - Tell them that a printed menu for a party, sitting on a plate stand for a buffet, is a nice touch. For a sit-down meal, place a menu at each place. These are easy to do on the computer on nice card stock and they always bring a sense of elegance to the occasion.

Menu
Fruit Skewers
Finger Sandwiches
Open-Faced Tea Fruit Sandwiches
Cream Cheese & Cucumber Sandwiches
Egg Salad Sandwiches
Chicken and Blueberry Salad Sandwiches
Chicken and Blueberry Sandwiches
Apricot Chicken Salad Sandwiches
Bacon-Cheddar Scones

Chocolate Scones
Mini Muffins
Chocolate Chocolate-Chip Zucchini Bread
Russian Tea Cookies
Lemon Drop Cookies
Graham Caramel Chunks
White Chocolate - Cranberry Cookies
Tea / Coffee / Sugar cubes / Milk

5. **Guest Book Page** - Have the girls take a piece of paper and adhere to card-stock. They can write guests at the top and underline it. They can give it to you to put in the box for the party so they don't forget it or put it in their binder to bring the day of the party. These will be their "guest books". At the party, they can ask everyone to sign it or write a little note. What a nice memory it will be, maybe with a picture attached of all the moms and daughters.

6. **Polishing Silver** - Use Wright's Brand Silver Cream. Have some tarnished pieces of silver out with cloths with which the girls can polish the pieces. Have girls wear cleaning gloves while they polish. These can be purchased inexpensively at a dollar store. This should be done over a sink. Trays, coffee pitchers, sugar cube spoon or tongs, creamer and sugar would be the main pieces needed for a tea. If possible, ask the mom who will host the tea to bring hers so it can be polished for the big party. Silver is certainly not necessary for the tea but learning how to polish silver is important.

7. **Table and Place Settings** - For this party, the food will all be finger food so the only utensils we will need are teaspoons. Your place setting should have a napkin to the left, a luncheon size plate which is between a bread plate and a dinner plate, and a small knife for spreading jams and curds which goes to the right of the plate with blade facing in, and a teaspoon to the right of the plate. Remember moms are bringing their own tea cups, otherwise, that would be placed to the right of the napkin. The center will have cream and sugar at both ends of the table, butter and an assortment of jams although they could be placed on a buffet with the breads if the tea is being served that way. Finally, the centerpiece should be a grouping of pineapples as this is the symbol for hospitality. Always work in odd numbers when arranging items on a table so use 1, 3, 5... depending on the size of the table. Either group them in the center or place one every so often down a long table to break up the length.

8. **Games** - Every party is more fun when planned games take place. It is a nice way to organize everyone from different places into one common activity. Since this is a tea, it would be fun to do feminine games related to this theme but fun for the girls to see their moms participate in. Games are usually played after the

food is served and eaten but doesn't have to be then. If time allows, play a couple of games at the meeting with the girls to "preview" what they will be doing at the party after the serving part is done.

1) **Jewelry Pass Relay** - Divide into three teams depending on how many girls and moms there are. Form three lines and have a dish of "jewels" and a high heel at the beginning of each line. (The jewels can be the flat marbles used in flower arranging or aquariums or other like stone.) Place a "jewelry box" at the end of each line. The game begins with the first person in each line scooping up one jewel with the high heel and passing it down the line to the last person who places it in the jewelry box. The high heel remains with the first girl and only one jewel can be passed at a time. The first team to get all their jewels into their jewelry box wins. (If someone passes more than one jewel at a time, the penalty is adding two extra jewels to their dish at the beginning of the line.)

2) **Dress-Up Relay -** Have a pile of tea clothes including things like gloves, high heels, hat, scarf, boa for each team. The first person runs down and puts everything on including heels and swiftly returns to the next in line. She takes it off and the next girl puts it on, runs to the end, takes it off and runs back, etc. until everyone has done it. If each girl sits down once she is done, it is easiest to see that they are complete. If it's a nice day, this can be done outside.

8. **Job Assignments -** Make a list of who will serve and clear, clean ahead of time, clean up after and do dishes. Put in box with things to pass on to Hostess for Tea.

Conclusion: Tell the girls what a wonderful job they have done in preparing for their moms. Remind them of a few things they will have to bring the day of the party: their aprons, their assigned dishes, their guest list page, their mom, tea cup and themselves! Talk about the importance of always remembering why we entertain others. It is a lot of fun but we want to center it on the practice of the virtue of hospitality: serving others and seeing Christ in everyone we meet.

NOTES TO MOM HOSTING TEA

Have girls come ahead to help clean and set the table or buffet. Look over notes from this month to see the decorations especially the pineapple centerpieces. Please have the girls prepare, clean before and after, serve and clear and keep an eye on replenishing the dishes. Of course, you or another mom may want to set out the coffee and tea so no one gets burned.

Remind the girls of their manners and the reason they are here for the tea: to make their moms feel special. It is not a party that they are attending, they are the hostesses, the servers. Their moms are the guests.

Have fun above all else. This is a wonderful day for friendship and enjoying the good things we have been given with others.

TAKE HOME

This month review your books as you will be practicing all your skills. The only thing this month to prepare is your assigned recipes for the party. Remember to bring your apron, dress appropriately (no jeans or t-shirts), bring your recipe and mark the bottom of the plate with masking tape and name, bring your mom and remind her to bring her favorite tea cup and baby picture. Remember the skills you've learned all year. "Do unto others as you would have them do unto you."

Recommended Reading
On the Banks of Plum Creek by Laura Ingalls Wilder
Aunt Jo's Scrap Bag by Louisa May Alcott

Recommended Movies
Meet Me in St. Louis with Judy Garland - This has some great party scenes and shows all the planning that goes into the big World's Fair at the end of the movie.

Recipes for Tea

Open-Faced Tea Fruit Sandwiches
Creamy Peanut Butter
Cream Cheese or Mascarpone Cheese
Ritz Crackers or Healthy version
Round Graham Crackers or Vanilla or Chocolate Wafer Cookies
Fruit Slices- Strawberries, kiwi, apple, pear, peaches or small berries

Directions: Spread peanut butter onto graham cracker rounds or wafer cookie.
Spread cream cheese or mascarpone cheese onto Ritz type crackers;
Top with sliced apples (dipped in lemon juice to prevent browning), kiwi slices,
and other fruit slices.

Fruit Skewers
Pineapple chunks
Strawberries
Melons, cubed
Cheese cubes - cheddar, havarti or mozzarella
Poppy Seed, raspberry vinaigrette or other sweet dressing
Toothpicks

Directions: Thread chunks of cheese alternating with fruit on toothpick skewers.
Serve with dressing as dip on side or pour gently over top of all.

Cream Cheese Sandwiches
Cream Cheese, softened or in the tub
Cucumbers, thinly sliced
Salt
White Bread
Dill, freshly cut or dried
Flower Cookie Cutters, optional

Directions: Remove all crust from bread. Cut out with cookie cutter for pretty shapes,
otherwise, cut in triangles when done. Spread with cream cheese. Place cucumbers on
cream cheese, sprinkle with salt and dill and top with second piece of bread. If not
using cutters, then slice sandwich at a diagonal both ways to create 4 triangle sandwiches.

Egg Salad Sandwiches (Makes 16 sandwiches, 64 finger sandwiches)
16 Boiled eggs, peeled and mashed
4-5 Tablespoons Dijon mustard
1 1/2 cup Mayonnaise
1 tsp. Salt
32 pieces of white bread, crusts cut off

Directions: Mash peeled hard boiled eggs with fork or potato masher. Mix in mayonnaise and mustard, salt. Check seasonings. Trim off crust of bread. Spread each piece with egg salad and top with another piece of bread. Cut in diagonals both ways to make 4 triangle sandwiches. Plate with parsley in center. (Save some egg salad in a small dish with some rice crackers for those who can not eat bread.)

Chicken and Blueberry Sandwiches
4 cups cooked and chopped chicken breasts (can used canned white chicken)
1 cup thin sliced celery, small cuts
2/3 cup mayonnaise
2 tsp. grated lemon peel
¼ tsp. each: salt and pepper
2 cup blueberries, fresh not frozen
20 or so mini croissants preferably or small dinner rolls (these are easy to find at store)

Directions: Mix chicken, mayonnaise, lemon peel, salt and pepper. Gently fold in blueberries. Slice croissants in half but not all the way through. Spread salad onto each. Fold over top. Plate and serve.

Apricot Chicken Salad
½ cup light sour cream
2 tbsp. apricot preserves and lemon juice
1 ½ cups chopped cooked chicken (cook your own or buy rotisserie chicken and use meat)
½ cup sliced dried apricots
¼ cup diced purple or sweet onion, optional
Cracker of choice

Directions: Mix sour cream, preserves and lemon juice in medium bowl. Add chopped chicken and apricots, (onion if using). Cover. Refrigerate overnight or until chilled. Serve on crackers.

Bacon-Cheddar Scones (2)

2 cups flour
2 tsp. baking powder
¼ cup (½ stick) cold butter
3 eggs, 2 for recipe, one for top
½ cup half-and-half
1 ½ cup shredded cheddar cheese
8 slices cooked bacon
1 tbsp. water

Directions: Preheat oven to 425 degrees. Mix flour and baking powder in large bowl. Cut in the butter with fork or pastry blender. (Can also be pulsed in food processor). Add 2 of the eggs and cream; mix until well blended. Add to flour mixture; stir just until moistened. Stir in cheese and crumbled bacon. Shape into ball. Knead dough on lightly floured surface about 10 times. Roll out to 12x6-inch rectangle. Cut into 8 (3-inch) squares; cut each diagonally in half. Place on lightly greased baking sheet. Beat remaining egg and the water and brush over triangles. Bake for 14-16 minutes until lightly browned.

Chocolate Scones

2 ½ cups all purpose flour
½ cup unsweetened cocoa powder
½ cup sugar
2 tsp. baking powder
½ tsp salt
½ cup (1 stick) chilled butter, cut into ½ inch cubes
1 ¼ cups chilled whipping cream
1 large egg yolk
Cream or whole milk for top
Raspberry jam

Directions: Preheat oven to 425 degrees. Whisk flour, cocoa powder, sugar, baking powder, and salt in large bowl to blend. Rub in butter with fingertips until coarse meal forms. Whisk egg yolk and cream in small bowl and stir into flour mixture to blend. Transfer to lightly floured surface. I use a big cutting board lined with wax paper and sprinkled with flour. Knead the dough 5 times or so to bring the dough into a ball. Pat into rectangle about ¾ inch thick and cut into 3 pieces across width. Cut each of these three pieces into 3 pieces and cut these at a diagonal to form triangles. Brush tops with cream or whole milk. Bake scones about 19 minutes until puffed around edges.

Chocolate-Chocolate-Chip Zucchini Bread

3 eggs
1 cup brown sugar
1 cup white sugar
1 cup oil or butter, melted
1 tsp. vanilla
1 tsp. each: cinnamon, salt, baking soda
¼ tsp. baking powder
2 cups shredded zucchini
3 cups flour
¼ cup unsweetened chocolate powder
1 cup mini chocolate chips

Directions: Preheat oven 350 degrees. Beat eggs until foamy. Add sugars, oil or butter, vanilla, cinnamon, salt and the rest of the ingredients. Mix well. Turn into 2 greased 5x9 loaf pans. Bake for 1 hour-1 hour and 20minutes. Check with skewer to see if it comes out clean. Cool and slice.

Russian Tea Surprise Cookies

1 cup butter
2 ¼ cups all purpose flour
1/3 cup sugar
1 tsp. vanilla
1 cup chopped pecans
½ bag chocolate kisses
1 cup sifted powdered sugar

Directions: Preheat oven to 325 degrees. In a mixing bowl beat butter for 30 seconds. Add half of the flour, the sugar and 1 tablespoon of water. Beat until thoroughly combined. Beat in remaining flour. Stir in pecans (can be left out if nut allergy). Unwrap chocolate kisses and take a tablespoon or so of dough and form around chocolate kiss to form a ball. Place on ungreased cookie sheet for about 20 minutes until bottoms are slightly browned. Cool cookies on wire rack. Gently shake and coat cooled cookies in bag filled with the cup of powdered sugar, use more if necessary. Makes about 30 cookies.

Lemon Drop Cookies

1 cup sugar
½ cup butter
½ cup sour cream or plain yogurt
2 eggs

2 tsp. grated lemon peel
4 tsp. juice of lemon
2 ½ cups flour
1 tsp. baking powder
½ tsp. salt
Glaze
1 cup powdered sugar
1-2 tbsp. juice of lemon

Directions:Combine sugar and butter. Cream for 2 minutes. Add sour cream or yogurt, eggs, lemon peel and juice. Continue beating until well combined, about 2 minutes. Reduce speed to low and add flour, baking powder and salt. Mix for 1-2 minutes. Drop dough by rounded teaspoons 2 inches apart on a greased cookie sheet or silpat. Cook for 10-12 minutes. Cool on rack and glaze when cooled.

Graham Caramel Chunks

Honey Grahams or other graham cracker bites
1 cup butter
1 cup brown sugar
1 cup chopped walnuts
1- 1 ½ cups chocolate chips or chopped-up chocolate

Directions: Preheat oven to 350 degrees. Combine butter and brown sugar in large pyrex or bowl. Microwave on high for 2 minutes. Stir. Microwave another 1 ½ - 2 minutes. Meanwhile, lay out grahams on cookie sheet or fill sheet. When caramel is done, working quickly, stir until smooth and spread over grahams. Top with chopped nuts. Bake for 6-8 minutes or until lightly browned and bubbly. Sprinkle with chocolate chips and bake an additional 2 minutes. Cool and break into chunks.

Triple-Chocolate Cranberry Oatmeal Cookies

2 cup flour
1 tsp. baking soda
1 tsp. cinnamon
½ tsp. salt
2 ½ sticks butter
1 cup sugar
1 cup brown sugar
2 large eggs
2 tsp. vanilla
2 cup old-fashioned oats
1 cup semi-sweet chocolate chips
1 cup milk chocolate chips

1 cup white chocolate chips
1 cup dried cranberries
2 ounces milk chocolate or white chocolate, chopped (for icing)

Directions: Preheat oven to 350 degrees. Whisk flour, baking soda, cinnamon, and salt in medium bowl to blend. Using mixer, beat butter and both sugars in large bowl until smooth. Beat in egg and vanilla. Add flour mixture and oats and stir until blended. Stir in all chocolate chips and cranberries. Drop by rounded tablespoons onto cookie sheets 2 inches apart. Bake cookies for 16 minutes. Cool 5 minutes on sheets and transfer to rack. Cool completely. Stir 2 ounces of chocolate in top of double boiler. (I take a glass bowl and set it in a saucepan that has 1 ½ cups or so of water brought to a simmer. The bowl acts as a double boiler and melts the chocolate smoothly.) Using small spoon, drizzle melted chocolate over cookies in zig-zag pattern. Cookies will set in about an hour or transfer to fridge to harden faster if necessary.

Hospitality: Book Club on Eight Cousins By Louisa May Alcott

"Teach me knowledge and good judgment." Psalm 119:66

Holy Inspiration: Our Lord tells us that as we do unto others, we do unto Him. Let us remember this in our conversations today. Include everyone, listen to everyone, be kind to everyone. In this way, we will be serving each other and being truly hospitable both as guests and as true "little women."

Our Lady's Patronage: Our Lady of the Epiphany will be our intercessor for our book club. Like the Wise Men to whom Christ manifested (literal meaning of "epiphany") Himself, we hope to still be wise men and little women as we seek knowledge of Christ. Discussing literature is a valuable way to learn how to logically analyze the world around us. This is the first step in acquiring wisdom. Our Lady of Epiphany, give us the grace to see all through the eyes of Christ.

Literature Example: Instead of a passage from literature, today we will have read a wonderful book about a girl who was trained to be skilled in all the areas that we have. Rose, the main character in *Eight Cousins*, is a wonderful model for us to get to know, to understand the true compassion she had for others, and how she accomplished bringing hospitality to them while still having fun. She showed us how to enjoy all that the true good life allows. The good life is living a life of skill, virtue, and faith. This is the life Our Lord wants for all of us.

Show the girls a map and locate Massachusetts so they know where the story takes place. It's a lot more fun to visit places that we have seen before through our books. The New England states, especially the Boston, Massachusetts area where Louisa May Alcott's stories take place, are still beautiful and fun to visit. It is the place of many of our founding fathers, the pilgrims' first colonies and so much history of our country.

Charm: Book

Discussion: Introduce the book by telling the girls this is a wonderful book about learning the skills to become a happy and learned lady. We see the virtue that develops in the main character as she acquires each skill and through her love she gives to those around her.

This book discussion is a time everyone gets to practice the skills we have learned: our manners and genuine hospitality towards each other. Let us listen to each other, try not to interrupt and enjoy each other's friendship. This is an opportunity to serve each other. If someone does not say much or have an opportunity to speak, try to include them. Ask them their opinion or favorite part. It is more important how we act towards each other than what we always say, although we want to speak of things that are interesting and wholesome.

Begin the Discussion:

1. Let the girls discuss their impressions of the book; how did they like it?

2. What virtues did Rose develop?

3. How did she practice the skill of hospitality?

These are some guides for the hostess, but let the girls try to lead the discussion.

a. She was generous to others

1) The boat party is a good example of this when she stayed behind and let the little maid have a holiday. She did her jobs for her without complaining so that her friend, the maid, could have a wonderful day. Near the end of the day, the reader could see it was hard on her to miss the fun but she persevered.

2) She sacrificed for her cousins remembering her aunt's words that she had to better them. She took out her earrings knowing that her holes would close up as a promise in exchange for the cousins to give up smoking. This was a very difficult thing for her to do especially since her uncle had given her the ring earrings. She put them on the boys' fingers as a reminder of their promise.

b. She was always grateful especially to her uncle for all he did for her. When she had to choose who to live with at the end of the story, she chose her uncle as he had given her so much love.

c. She brought hospitality to others - Each time she changed houses to stay with a different aunt, she tried to bring happiness to that house. One of the clearest examples of this was the joy she brought to her very ill cousin who could do very little in his condition. She read to him and helped him to not fall too far behind in his studies during his absence.

Conclusion: Once the girls are done discussing the book, end with a social hour to celebrate all the hard work they did this year.

ORDER FORM

Quantity	Description	Size/type	Unit Price	Total
	The Orphans Find a Home, A St. Cabrini story		$7.95	
	Fun with the Orphans, stories, games, crafts		$8.95	
	The Orphans Art and Activity Book		$3.95	
	Kat Finds a Friend, a St. Eliz Seton Story		$7.95	
	Kat's Play Book, puppets, games, plays		$8.95	
	Thomas Finds a Treasure, a St. John Neumann story		$7.95	
	Thomas' Art and Game Treasure Chest		$3.95	
	Willy Finds Victory, a Blessed Francis Seelos Story		$7.95	
	Little Women Hospitality Book-Teacher's Manual		$14.95	
	Little Women Hospitality Book-Student Guide		$5.95	
	Set of 10 Charms with 7.5 in bracelet		$22.95	
	Set of 10 Charms with 18 in necklace		$24.95	
	Set of 10 Charms		$19.95	
	Individual Charms (please specify)		$2.50	
	Little Flower's Girls' Club Leader's Guide Wreath I		$10.00	
	Little Flowers Girls' Club Member's Guide Wreath I		$4.50	
	Little Flowers Girls' Club Leader's Guide Wreath II		$10.00	
	Little Flowers Girls' Club Member's Guide Wreath II		$4.50	
	Little Flowers Girls' Club Leader's Guide Wreath III		$10.00	
	Little Flowers Girls' Club Member's Guide Wreath III		$4.50	
	Little Flowers Girls' Club t-shirts child (S-M-L)		$10.95	
	Little Flowers Girls' Club t-shirts adult (S-M-L-XL)		$15.95	
	Little Flowers Girls' Club Memory Verse CD		$12.00	
	Patch set Wreath I, II or III (specify set of 10 patches)		$10/set	
	Name Badge		$4.00	
	Sash-small ($4.95) large ($5.95) deluxe-lined ($12)		$4.95/$5.95/$12	
	Little Flowers Girls' Club Tea and Luncheon Manual		$4.95	
	Blue Knights Boys' Club Year I Leader's Guide		$10.00	
	Blue Knights Boys' Club Year I Member's Guide		$4.50	
	Blue Knights Boys' Club Year II Leader's Guide		$10.00	
	Blue Knights Boys' Club Year II Member's Guide		$4.50	
	Blue Knights Boys' Club Year III Leader's Guide		$10.00	
	Blue Knights Boys' Club Year III Member's Guide		$4.50	
	Blue Knights Boys' Club t-shirts child (s-M-L)		$10.95	
	Blue Knights Boy's Club t-shirts adult (SMLXL)		$15.95	

Payment: CC Number:_____-_____-_____-_____   Subtotal_____
        Expiration:___/____   Sales Tax (KY 6%)_____
        Signature_____   Shipping _____
        Check enclosed: _____   Total   _____

Shipping: $0-$30: $5.50
        $31-$50: $6.50
        $51-$75 $8.00
        $75-$100 $9.00
        $101 & up $10.00

Send order form: Ecce Homo Press, 6401 Shrader Ln., LaGrange, KY 40031

SHIP TO:
NAME:_____
ADDRESS_____
CITY:_____ST:_____ ZIP:_____
PHONE:(_____)_____

ORDER ONLINE at: www.eccehomopress.com or call toll free: 1-866-305-8362
Please call or check online for current prices and shipping charges.

NOTES:

NOTES:

120